The politics of Africa's economic stagnation

African states are not, in any real sense, capitalist states. Elsewhere, the state has played a crucial role in facilitating capitalist expansion, but in postcolonial Africa one finds a form of neopatrimonialism – personal rule – that introduces a variety of economic irrationalities. Productive economic activities are impeded by the political instability, systemic corruption and maladminstration associated with personal rule. In extreme cases, a downward spiral of political-economic decline is set in motion that is difficult to halt and reverse.

Is personal rule simply a euphemism for ineptitude and mismanagement? The authors argue that it is not; it operates according to a particular political rationality that shapes a ruler's actions when, in the absence of legitimate authority, he is confronted with the challenge of governing an unintegrated peasant society. Neopatrimonialism is essentially an adaptation of colonial-inspired political institutions to peculiar historical and social conditions.

This book focuses on the political factor as an important cause of Africa's economic ills. It analyses the social conditions impelling political adaptation and the consequences of personal rule for economic life, and surveys creative responses to the predicament African people now face.

AFRICAN SOCIETY TODAY

General editor: ROBIN COHEN

Advisory editors: O. Aribiah, Jean Copans,
Paul Lubeck, Philip M. Mbithi, M. S. Muntemba,
O. Nnoli, Richard Sandbrook

The series has been designed to provide scholarly, but lively and up-to-date, books, likely to appeal to a wide readership. The authors will be drawn from the field of development studies and all the social sciences, and will also have had experience of teaching and research in a number of African countries.

The books will deal with the various social groups and classes that comprise contemporary African society and successive volumes will link with previous volumes to create an integrated and comprehensive picture of the African social structure.

Also in the series

Farm labour. KEN SWINDELL
Migrant laborers. SHARON STICHTER

THE POLITICS OF AFRICA'S ECONOMIC STAGNATION

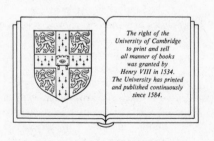

RICHARD SANDBROOK

with

JUDITH BARKER

The right of the
University of Cambridge
to print and sell
all manner of books
was granted by
Henry VIII in 1534.
The University has printed
and published continuously
since 1584.

CAMBRIDGE UNIVERSITY PRESS

Cambridge

London   New York   New Rochelle
Melbourne   Sydney

Published by the Press Syndicate of the University of Cambridge
The Pitt Building, Trumpington Street, Cambridge CB2 1RP
32 East 57th Street, New York, NY 10022, USA
10 Stamford Road, Oakleigh, Melbourne 3166, Australia

© Cambridge University Press 1985

First published 1985

Printed in Great Britain at the University Press, Cambridge

Library of Congress catalogue card number: 84-28588

British Library Cataloguing in Publication Data
Sandbrook, Richard
The politics of Africa's economic stagnation
(African society today)
1. Africa—Social conditions
I. Title   II. Barker, Judith   III. Series
960'.328   HN773.5

Library of Congress Cataloging in Publication Data
Sandbrook, Richard.
The politics of Africa's economic stagnation.
(African society today)
Bibliography: p.
Includes index.
1. Africa—Economic conditions—1960- .
2. Africa—Politics and government—1960- .
3. Africa—Social conditions—1960- I. Barker,
Judith. II. Title. III. Series.
HC800.S26 1985   960'.328   84-28588

ISBN 0 521 26587 8
ISBN 0 521 31961 7 (pbk.)

SE

CONTENTS

TABLES

ACKNOWLEDGEMENTS

This is a well-travelled book, and it has incurred many debts in the course of its journey. The Social Sciences and Humanities Research Council of Canada (SSHRCC) awarded the research grant for study in the Ivory Coast, Kenya and the Sudan in November-December 1983 and also funded earlier research and study in Kenya, Ghana and Nigeria. A sabbatical leave fellowship from the SSHRCC also supported a five-month stay in 1984 at the Centre de Recherche et d'Étude sur les Pays d'Afrique Orientale (CREPAO) at the University of Pau, France. Here, we consulted some of the voluminous French literature on African development and undertook much of the actual writing.

Financial support is important to an enterprise such as this; so too are the assistance, encouragement and constructive criticism of many individuals. Friends and colleagues in the Ivory Coast, Kenya and the Sudan aided my investigations in these countries, but my thanks to them is best given privately. In France, Professor François Constantin, head of CREPAO, facilitated my research and organized a day-long colloquium in Pau at the end of May 1984 on the topic of this book: 'L'état africain en crise: La personnalisation du pouvoir et la stagnation capitaliste'. This provided me with a very useful critique; especially helpful were Denis C. Martin, an Africanist at the Centre d'Études et de Recherches Internationales at the Paris-based Fondation Nationale des

Sciences Politiques, Jean Copans of the Centre d'Études Africaines at École des Hautes Études en Sciences Sociales in Paris, Yves Fauré of the Centre d'Études d'Afrique Noire at the University of Bordeaux, and Frank Moderne and François Constantin of CREPAO in Pau. Maryse Leisure, Professor of French at the Universities of Pau and California (Santa Barbara), not only laboured to improve my French facility, but proved herself a good friend by assisting the adjustment of my family and me to French life.

Various people at the University of Toronto also played an important role. Toru Kotani, a Ph.D. student, was an exemplary research assistant throughout 1983, unearthing an unending supply of relevant documents and studies and summarizing or evaluating some of them. My colleagues in the Development Studies Programme's study group on The State and Development Strategies in 1983 stimulated new lines of thought on this complex subject. My most profound intellectual debt is to my friend Cranford Pratt who, in his usual tactful yet frank manner, provided a trenchant critique of an earlier draft of this book.

R.S.

GLOSSARY

All the terms marked by an asterisk (*) in the text are included in this glossary. Words which are adequately defined in the text generally do not appear here.

BALANCE OF PAYMENTS CRISIS. Occurs when a country suffers a large decline in its net foreign income (owing to world recession, a loss of former competitive advantages in international trade, mismanagement, etc.) and thus runs a continual deficit on its current account of visible and invisible trade. This situation requires remedial action. Members of the INTERNATIONAL MONETARY FUND can draw upon its financial resources to balance their accounts while they restructure their economies.

CAPITAL ACCUMULATION. The formation of a fund of capital investment to expand production. This is different from savings *per se*. 'Real' accumulation is not simply the accumulation of money resources; it is the use of these to augment or replace fixed assets.

ECONOMIC SURPLUS. Identical with current saving. It is the difference between current output and current consumption during a particular period.

EXTERNALITIES. The costs and benefits which are not reflected in market prices. If the net balance of these costs and benefits is positive there is an external economy; if the net balance is negative, there is an external diseconomy.

FORMAL (OR MODERN) SECTOR. Includes those economic activities that show up in a country's labour statistics. This excludes very small businesses, most self-employment, odd jobs, and illegal activities, which together constitute the informal sector.

GROSS DOMESTIC PRODUCT (GDP). A measure of the total productive activity of a country's economy during a particular year. It represents the value of the total output of goods and services produced by both residents and non-residents in the domestic economy, regardless of the allocation of income between these two categories.

GROSS NATIONAL PRODUCT (GNP). A measure of the total productive activity of a country's population, both at home and abroad, during a particular year. It represents the value of the total output of goods and services produced by a society, excluding the income earned in the domestic economy by non-residents and including income received by residents from abroad.

INFRASTRUCTURE. All the facilities and services provided by the state which, though not directly productive, are essential to the productivity of the economy. These include services that both directly facilitate production (transport and telecommunications facilities, electricity and water) and indirectly assist productivity by fostering a skilled, healthy, motivated labour force (schools, technical education, sanitation, sports and health facilities).

INSTITUTION, POLITICAL AND ADMINISTRATIVE. A valued and stable procedural rule or organizational device for resolving disputes, selecting leaders and making authoritative decisions.

INTERNATIONAL MONETARY FUND (IMF). An organization of 143 member countries, with its headquarters in Washington, D.C., whose role is to make financing available to members suffering BALANCE OF PAYMENTS CRISES and provide technical economic assistance. The IMF's resources derive mainly from members' subscriptions (geared to relative economic size), borrowings and sales of its gold stock. A member may draw up to the amount of its quota from the fund and, if in severe difficulties, up to 140 per cent of its quota with repayment over ten years. However, the IMF attaches stringent conditions regarding economic policies before granting an 'extended' facility.

INTRAFIRM TRADE. Trade between branches of the same transnational corporation but located in different national jurisdictions. The absence of an 'arm's-length' relationship between the trading partners increases the likelihood that they may collude to further the global profit considerations of the parent corporation, at the expense of the national economic goals of one or more host governments.

MARKETING BOARDS. Established by statute (see PARASTATALS) to eliminate or minimize the middleman's role in agriculture. These boards determine the producer's price for various commodities. Their purpose is to stabilize producer prices, thus reducing risks and encouraging investment, though in practice governments have often used them to tax the producer and subsidize the (domestic) consumer.

MONOPSONY. Exists when a single firm or collaborating group of firms is the sole buyer of a commodity being sold by a large number of independent producers. The danger is that the buyer will offer a purchase price below that which would be determined by market forces and will gain control over key decisions regarding production itself.

PARASTATALS. Statutory boards and publicly-controlled corporations which in principle retain some measure of autonomy from governmental direction on a day-to-day basis. Boards are responsible for regulation (e.g., licensing boards), the operation of public utilities, social services and credit facilities, and commodity buying and selling. Public corporations, which may or may not be established by statute, operate like conventional holding companies and firms. The government exercises a varying degree of control by the appointment of a majority of directors and often the chief executive officers as well.

STATE. A centralized and hierarchical system of authority relations within a given territory that depends ultimately for its survival on a monopoly of legitimate coercion.

TECHNOLOGY. The tools, equipment and materials used in the production process and the products which are the output. It also includes an unembodied component – the technical and organizational skills needed to make efficient use of the hardware. Technological dependence exists when a society must continually rely upon the technical innovations and knowhow of foreigners for its technical progress.

TRANSNATIONAL CORPORATIONS. A corporation that is usually controlled by the nationals of a single country but itself controls or operates productive facilities in two or more countries.

WORLD BANK. Consists of the International Bank for Reconstruction and Development (IBRD), established in 1945, and the International Development Association (IDA), created in 1960. Both organizations share the same staff and headquarters in Washington, D.C. There are currently 143 member countries. Funded largely by borrowings on the international capital markets, the IBRD makes loans at slightly above the lowest commercial rate to assist development programmes in developing countries. The IDA dispenses concessionary loans to the world's poorest countries – a total of $US 2.7 billion to 42 countries in 1982.

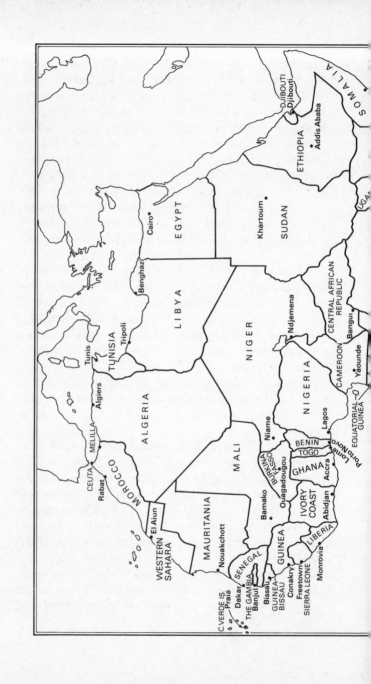

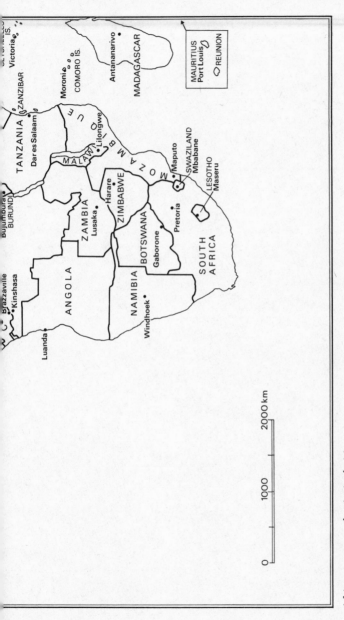

African states and principal cities

§1§

DISAPPOINTMENTS OF
INDEPENDENCE

> I plead sickness,
> I am an orphan,
> I am diseased with
> All the giant
> Diseases of Society,
> Crippled by the cancer
> Of Uhuru
> Far worse than
> The yaws of
> Colonialism,
> The walls of hopelessness
> Surround me completely,
> There are no windows
> To let in the air
> Of hope!
>
> Okot p'Bitek, *Song of Prisoner*, p. 50

Democracy, prosperity and self-rule – this was the vision of African independence. But today, few Africans express satisfaction with the fruits of *uhuru*. Those heady days of anti-colonial mobilization, demonstrations and demands, though only three decades old, seem now a dream from which one has awakened to another historical epoch. What went wrong?

For Western students of Africa, the disappointment is largely of our own making. Our expectations in the 1960s were too grand, too romantic and profoundly unfair. Surely, we thought, the sufferings of the African people would give birth to a new man, a man of virtue committed to collective betterment and democracy. But exploitation and powerlessness do not create any special virtue. Sceptics now, we endorse the novelist Ayi Kwei Armah's lament – 'The Beautyful Ones are not yet Born'.

A more positive view is expressed by professional developmentalists employed by international agencies. Publicly, they speak of Africa's problems, but also of the 'vast potential' of nations bubbling with 'the ferment of development'. Privately, however, they are generally less sanguine.

For something has gone wrong. The symptoms of Africa's economic crisis are legion: nil or negative rates of increase in Gross Domestic Product* per capita; decline in the export of primary products and in agricultural productivity; underutilization of a modest industrial plant; severe balance of payments deficits; worsening income inequality; and more extensive absolute poverty. Moreover, this crisis cannot be attributed solely to the recent world recession. Even in the halcyon days of the 1960s and 1970s, African economies as a group performed poorly in comparison to Latin American or East Asian ones. Another dimension of crisis is political decay, evident in widespread corruption, bureaucratic immobilism, political violence and instability. This deterioration of the state signifies, among other things, a diminished capacity to rescue ailing national economies when the world economic climate improves.

Ghana provides an apt portrait of this deterioration, though the government's adherence to a strict deflationary programme since early 1983 holds out hope for a long-term improvement. The first colony to win independence, Ghana emerged as a sovereign nation in 1957 with living standards, infrastructure* and administrative competence unequalled in Black Africa. But its economy has been in decline since the 1960s.[1] In the 1970s, per capita Gross Domestic Product* fell more than three per cent per annum. Output declined in all major sectors – cocoa, timber, mining and manufacturing. Annual price inflation averaged 50–100 per cent. Ghanaian currency (the cedi) traded on the black market at 10 to 20 times below the official rate (until a major devaluation in April 1983). While the modern economy collapsed, *kalabule* – the Ghanaian term for the black market or parallel economy – flourished.

The human dimensions of this economic crisis were tragic. A labourer had to work for more than a day to buy a beer, and almost two days to buy a loaf of bread. In 1983, a yam sufficient for a family meal cost as much as 200 cedis, or two weeks' wages for a labourer. In addition, households were obliged to waste a great deal of time each day locating supplies, as food and other essential commodities were scarce. The shelves of large shops were woefully barren. Only at black market prices were spare parts and other machinery available.

The deterioration of public services compounded the decline in living standards. Frequent interruptions in the supply of electricity and water to the towns were both annoying and economically destructive. Although deteriorating roads were often impassable in the rainy season, they were not repaired. Only 30 per cent of the truck and bus fleet and 20 per cent of locomotives were serviceable in early 1983, according to a World Bank estimate. These problems delayed the transport of cocoa and foodstuffs to the cities and discouraged agricultural production. Hospitals, universities and schools also fell apart as professionals emigrated in search of a more agreeable life.

But economic hardship was only one aspect of the chaos. Ghanaians also suffered a heightening of personal insecurity; robbery and crimes of violence escalated and legal safeguards and civil liberties decayed. As the 1970s wore on, increasing numbers migrated to Nigeria, the Ivory Coast,

Europe, and North America, in order to escape this precarious existence.

Not all of Africa, by any means, has gone the way of Ghana. Subsaharan or tropical Africa – that part of the continent and nearby islands lying south of the Sahara but excluding the Republic of South Africa – is an immense region of 47 independent countries and 360 million people. There is inevitably much variation. Nonetheless, a precarious daily existence similar to that in Ghana prevails in many countries, for example in Angola, Chad, Equatorial Guinea, Ethiopia, Mozambique, Sudan, Uganda, Tanzania and Zaire. Civil war and drought have exacerbated already significant problems in most of these countries. Social and economic deterioration are not as marked in Botswana, Gabon, the Ivory Coast, Kenya and Malawi, all of which achieved respectable rates of GDP growth until the late 1970s. Yet these countries too faced immense challenges in the 1980s. For instance, *Business Environment Risk Index*, a US publication, warned its clients in 1982 against investing in the Ivory Coast, a favoured recipient of World Bank* and International Monetary Fund* (IMF) assistance, on the grounds that 'risks are substantial and profit opportunities limited', aside from petroleum.

Sadly, certain major trends spell long-term economic crisis in subsaharan Africa, the poorest region of the world's least developed continent. Of the 34 countries included in the World Bank's list of low-income economies (i.e., the least developed) in its 1984 *World Development Report*, fully 21 are tropical African countries. The grim patterns were evident twenty years ago. Only nine of 39 countries for which data exists achieved a 2.5 per annum per capita growth rate in the sixties and seventies (Table 1), and three of these were oil exporters. Fifteen economies registered a negative economic growth rate in the sevenites and, by the end of that decade, even such erstwhile high performers as

Table 1. *Socio-economic data, subsaharan Africa*

	Low-income countries (24)	Middle-income oil importers (11)	Middle-income oil exporters (4)
Population			
(millions mid-1979)	187.1	65.2	91.6
GNP* per capita	239.0	532.0	669.0
($US 1979)			
Annual Growth Rates (%)			
GNP per capita, 1960–79	0.9	1.5	3.2
Agriculture, 1970–9	1.5	3.5	−0.3
Industry, 1970–9	1.5	3.5	10.6
Labour Force			
1960–70	2.0	2.3	1.7
1970–80	2.1	2.6	1.7
1980–2000	2.8	3.1	3.2
Urban Population			
1960–70	5.8	5.3	4.7
1970–80	6.5	6.2	4.8
Food Production, per capita			
1977–9 (1969–71 = 100)	91.0	95.0	86.0

Notes: Weighted averages are used.
'Low-income countries' are those with a per capita income of less than $US 370.
Six subsaharan countries (all very small) are excluded due to lack of data.
Source: Statistical Annex, in World Bank's *Accelerated Development in Subsaharan Africa* (Washington, D.C., August 1981), various tables.

the Ivory Coast, Nigeria, Kenya and Malawi were beset with economic woes.

And what of the future? The prospects are bleak. No growth in per capita incomes is projected for low-income

African countries in the decade after 1985, according to the World Bank's 1983 *World Development Report*, even under the most optimistic assumptions.

Agriculture, the livelihood of 60 to 90 per cent of African national populations, has performed dismally. Previously self-sufficient in foodstuffs, Africa saw its population growth outstrip food production between 1960 and 1980. Indeed, the subsaharan experience is unique – the only region in the world where per capita food production actually fell during this era. The result is, of course, a growing need to import food. By the year 2000, tropical Africa will probably import one-third of its food requirements. Even the production of export crops has slumped in the seventies, ending the increases in output of the sixties. The implications are catastrophic for countries depending on the export of primary commodities for their foreign exchange.

Most impressive has been the overall industrial growth in the seventies: 13 of 34 reporting countries experienced annual rates of over five per cent. But statistics can mislead. The small industrial base on which these rates are calculated inflate the figures. The picture is also skewed by the 15 middle-income economies, particularly the oil exporters, which accounted disproportionately for industrial output. Finally, one must ask, is the pattern of industrial development appropriate? Manufacturing in this region typically relies upon capital, skill and import-intensive technologies provided by transnational corporations. Production is oriented mainly to the processing of primary exports and the local assembly or production of consumer goods for a relatively privileged minority. As the scale is small and the spin-offs few, minimal employment is created. And the modern manufacturing sector does not produce many goods to satisfy the basic needs of the majority; lacking purchasing power, the poor must have recourse to the cheaper and rougher goods produced by local artisans.

Severe balance of payments crises* were cropping up in all African countries by the mid to late 1970s. Shortfalls in foreign exchange can be accounted for by such factors as agricultural decline, worsening terms of trade with industrial countries (see Table 2), escalating oil bills and high interest rates on the foreign debt. The dimensions of this problem are attested to by Africa's rising world indebtedness: the external debt doubled between 1973 and 1977 and almost doubled again over the next four years to a whopping $US 56 billion, according to the International Monetary Fund's 1982 *Annual Report*. The Sudan's debt situation in 1984, though extreme, indicates just how desperate a balance of payments crisis can become. Burdened by a total debt equal to its GNP ($US 7 billion), Sudan would have needed to spend twice its export earnings just to service this debt. However, as the country's import bill was three times what it earned in exports, its debt continued to grow.

Absolute poverty has not declined significantly since independence. The economic difficulties provide part, but only part, of the explanation. Also significant is the pattern of growth, including in particular vast inequalities which current power structures perpetuate. Some countries – Kenya, Zambia, Nigeria, for instance – have experienced periods of robust economic growth, but these spurts afforded negligible relief of material deprivation.

Poverty is the number one social problem in tropical Africa. And its dimensions are very human. Two in ten children still die before their first birthdays. The life expectancy at 47 years is the lowest in the world. In all, 40 to 60 per cent of the subsaharan population is poor and this proportion is unlikely to diminish by 2000, studies by the World Bank, the International Labour Office and the Organization for Economic Cooperation and Development inform us.

In education and health care, however, Africa's achieve-

ments should be applauded. School enrolments have multiplied faster since the sixties than in any other region of the
Third World. By 1980, 63 per cent of the relevant age group
attended primary school in tropical Africa, a healthy
doubling of the proportion in twenty years. Health care
improvements have raised the life expectancy rate from 39
years in 1960 to the current 47.

But there are problems. Education is still generally oriented to the needs of that small minority who may find
employment in the modern, mainly urban, sector. Most
health-care budgets favour costly Western curative facilities
concentrated in the cities, at the expense of preventive
health care which caters to the rural majority. Although
such governments as Tanzania have tried to equalize access
to social services, backward regions remain extremely disadvantaged in most countries.

Income inequality is not, strictly speaking, an aspect of
economic crisis. Unequal distribution is common in the
early and middle stages of capitalist development, and
therefore is often linked with growth rather than stagnation. Nonetheless, the poor can tolerate inequity even less in
societies where the economic pie is constant or shrinking
than where it is expanding. If the rich get richer in the
former situation, other social classes clearly lose out. Social
tensions are, therefore, a dramatic concomitant of capitalist
stagnation.

The fact of vast inequalities in many subsaharan countries is tragically observable, but the data are scarce and
suspect.[2] In Gabon, Kenya, Zambia and Swaziland, the
distribution of income is among the most unequal in the
world. The concentration of income is apparently less
extreme, though still marked, in such other countries as
Ghana and Nigeria. The upper crust (usually the top 20 per
cent of the population) typically appropriates 60 per cent or
more of the national income. Courageous egalitarian poli-

cies to counteract this trend are seen in only a few cases, such as Tanzania and Mozambique, and at considerable economic cost.

Everywhere a gap exists between rural and urban incomes. The city promises most of the desirable jobs and lucrative opportunities in the public sector, commerce, real estate speculation and industry. Explosive rural–urban migration (Table 1) is a product of this urban bias along with stagnant or diminishing real incomes in small-scale agriculture. It is not unusual for a large African city to double its size every seven years; in the seventies, subsaharan urban areas grew at an annual rate of six per cent and the 35 major capitals expanded at a rate of 8.5 per cent. Indeed, by 1980, there were 28 subsaharan African cities of over 500,000 – a dramatic rise from the three 20 years before.

But the streets of the African city are not paved with gold. Most hopeful migrants from the country are sorely frustrated by what greets them beyond the core of the modern capital. One is struck by the incongruously intimate coexistence of the affluent suburbs and squalid slums, squatter settlements, or *bidonvilles*. The *nouveaux riches* fear the poor, for they see 40–50 per cent of their city's population subsisting in under-serviced, unsanitary, overcrowded settlements. Their residences become small fortresses, contained within rampart-like walls and guarded night and day by ferocious watchdogs and guards. Crimes against property are numerous, but ironically it is the undefended poor who inevitably bear the brunt of these attacks.

For most of subsaharan Africa, this disappointing record signifies the limitations of a particular attempt at capitalist development. One does not, of course, find here the classical pattern of capitalism with the predominance of private ownership and market relationships. Outside a small modern sector, peasant agriculture holds sway. The commercialization of agriculture is, therefore, only partial –

traditional land tenure hinders the development of land markets, traditional household labour obligations limit the growth of a rural proletariat and considerations of subsistence and household autonomy restrict production for the market. Even in the modern or formal sector,* the private capitalist firm is not the exclusive economic unit. It coexists with extensive public ownership in the form of wholly nationalized public corporations or joint ventures with private capital. And the state* also intervenes extensively to regulate markets – for example, by establishing monopsonistic marketing boards*, price controls on selected commodities and pegged exchange rates. Yet, for all this, a broadly capitalist framework guides the majority of African countries' attempts at growth. Extensive public intervention into economic life is, after all, a universal feature of contemporary capitalism. In Africa, the typically large dimensions of the public sector suggest that the prevalent approach is best described as state capitalism. Yet it is capitalism, nonetheless, for regimes place their faith, not in collectivist forms of agriculture or industry, but in the production of goods for the market by independent wage labour in accordance with profit considerations.

Not all of Africa is capitalist in orientation. A few regimes proclaim a commitment to Marxism-Leninism: Angola, Benin, Congo, Ethiopia, Guinea (until the death of Sékou Touré in 1984), Madagascar, Mozambique and Somalia. Ideological pronouncements notwithstanding, such regimes as Benin and Congo practice capitalism, albeit with a large public sector. And even formerly stalwart Marxist-Leninist Angola, Guinea, Mozambique and Somalia grew increasingly disillusioned with a collectivist strategy and/or Soviet tutelage in the late seventies or early eighties. Seeking a rapprochement with Western governments and investors, they all to a greater or lesser degree opened up their economies to market forces. Transnational corporations have long dominated Angola's oil industry and Guinea's bauxite production for example, but capitalist relations now also hold sway in other sectors including small-scale commerce and industry. Mozambique established links with the European Economic Community and edged away from its commitments to Soviet-style state farms; the Soviet Union, in retaliation, cut off economic aid in December 1983. Ethiopia remains stalwart in its Marxist-Leninist orientation. But even here the government has refrained from pressing collective farms in agriculture. And the dismal economic record of Ethiopia in the 1980s, even with Soviet assistance, is not such as to invite emulation.

Certain other regimes characterize themselves as socialist, though not necessarily Marxist-Leninist. Some of these, such as the Kenyatta regime in Kenya, have used African socialism only as a euphemistic cover for a transparently capitalist commitment. The psychological association of capitalism with colonialism is still too real to permit a wholehearted embrace. Other governments – those in the Cape Verde Islands, Guinea-Bissau, Mali, Tanzania, Zambia, Zimbabwe and Mauritius – have a stronger socialist commitment, but nonetheless allow considerable latitude for free enterprise.

Is capitalism then the best basis on which Africa can build its economic future? The widespread view that socialist experimentations have largely failed lends credence to this position. Of course, one might counter that many capitalist experiments have also gone awry. But the force of this argument is vitiated by the common attribution of capitalist failure to governments' fondness for public economic intervention – that is, to the supposedly socialist elements of a mixed-economy approach. Whatever the merits of this case, world recession and general economic decline clearly exert a firm pressure on African governments to free market forces and rely on private investment. All of them need desperately to obtain loans, aid and investment from international organizations, especially the IMF and the World Bank, bilateral agencies and private banks and corporations that favour such policies. Therefore, even socialist-oriented regimes are inexorably pushed in a capitalist direction as they seek a workable economic path in the midst of economic and, often, political chaos. Capitalism's potential in Africa thus remains a crucial question.

This is not only a question of which particular bundle of economic policies is likely to prove most effective in a certain country. Consideration of the appropriate degree of export orientation, the pros and cons of concentration on small-scale peasant agriculture, or the proper extent of reliance on direct foreign investment is of course necessary and valuable. But there is also a more fundamental question: how conducive is the African environment to capitalist development irrespective of particular policy approach? It is clear that capitalism in subsaharan Africa, in comparative Third-World terms, has not been particularly resilient and successful since 1960. Is this principally a matter of inadvisable policy formulation and implementation, or do more fundamental constraints operate?

We argue that the latter is the case and that socio-political factors, in particular, place severe limitations on economic development. Elsewhere the state has played a central role in capitalist development, indirectly through the generation of a conducive framework of political order and rational law and administration, and directly through the provision of adequate infrastructure, subsidies to promising firms and sectors and even productive public investment in strategic industries. But African states are not, in any real sense, capitalist states. The peculiar conditions of postcolonial Africa impel an adaptation of colonial-inspired political structures and processes in a patrimonial, or rather neopatrimonial, direction. The omnipresent danger in this adaptation is a degeneration of neopatrimonialism into an economically irrational form of 'personal rule'. This decay, manifest in political instability, systemic corruption and maladministration, introduces irrationalities into economic life, but nonetheless is shaped by a particular political logic. These political phenomena cannot, therefore, simply be dismissed as mismanagement or ineptitude.

Hence, a comprehension of the socio-political constraint on capitalism in Africa will take us far afield. It requires an analysis of the historical and social factors conditioning political adaptation, the logic of personal rule and the consequences of this for economic life. This is our task.

But politics is far from the only factor. Very real objective constraints also hinder capitalism in Africa. Let us investigate them now in order to place the socio-political factor in context.

❧ 2 ❧

WHY CAPITALISM FAILS

The obstacles confronting capitalism in Africa are major. Some believe these roadblocks are external in origin. A popular neo-Marxian thesis of the late 1960s and seventies attributed African underdevelopment to that continent's role in the world capitalist economy. This 'dependency' view contends that the international system spurred the advancement of imperialist centres at the expense of the underdeveloped periphery. This is denied by others, including certain Marxists, who emphasize internal problems: inappropriate attitudes, lack of skilled manpower, unavailability of local capital, scarce natural resources, overpopulation, mismanagement of public resources, and so on.[1]

In fact, both camps have a point. Yet rarely is either set of obstacles an impervious barrier to growth. Capitalism everywhere, including in Western Europe, has encountered obstructions. It is the task of creative political leadership to find ways around these. Unfortunately, the political life of tropical Africa usually discourages such a creative role. Too often, political elites fail to foster capitalist development and even inadvertently discourage it.

Internal impediments to growth are often major. The fact is that the raw economic potential of many African countries is negligible. It's not simply a matter of scarce natural resources – arable land, energy sources and mineral deposits. After all, such meagerly endowed countries as nineteenth-century Japan and contemporary South Korea, Singapore and Hong Kong have overcome these impediments and attained remarkable industrial growth. Particularly restrictive in Africa are such factors as harsh tropical environment and terrain, the tiny local market, a dearth of local managerial and technical skills and the general fragility of societies torn asunder by communal schisms.

Consider natural resources. First, arable land is not abundant in most countries. Much of Africa is desert and savannah – the Sahara Desert alone covers a quarter of the continent from the Atlantic to the Red Sea and creeps four miles southward each year. A lack of decent land is a growing problem for the rapidly expanding populations of countries like Nigeria, Kenya and those in the Sahel, where nearly three-quarters of the population depends on agriculture.[2] Droughts wreak periodic havoc on forty per cent of the arable land and the tsetse fly infests about 10 million square kilometres in 21 countries killing cattle with trypanosomiasis. Other parasites and disease kill and debilitate people: malaria and bilharzia, for instance, afflict nearly half of Africa's farmers. And the soils, once unprotected by ground cover, are fragile and easily eroded or depleted. All these factors obstruct the agricultural revolution which is a necessary condition for rapid industrial growth.

No discussion of Africa's economic problems is complete without a reference to the unprecedented climatic conditions that have recently prevailed. In mid-1984, no fewer than 31 subsaharan countries suffered drought, and famine afflicted one in every three people. Drought conditions had plagued the Sahelian countries since 1968 with little respite. There had also been three years of severely reduced rainfall in West Africa, the Horn of Africa, especially Ethiopia and

Somalia, and Southern Africa, including even Zimbabwe which is normally a net exporter of food. At a time when balance of payments was already in the red, the need to import large quantities of food placed an intolerable burden on faltering economies.

A second important resource is energy and minerals. These abound in some areas, but they are not always the godsends they may appear to be. Difficult terrain may render them prohibitively expensive to recover. Natural obstacles include a scarcity of natural harbours, few navigable rivers to the interior, the African plateau cut with deep valleys making road and railway construction extremely costly, and the fierce tropical rains that threaten the rapid erosion of road and railway. Therefore, the often massive investments that are required in transportation facilities militate against the exploitation of many natural resources.[3]

Petroleum deposits are a happier matter. The high unit value of petroleum means costly transportation poses less of a problem. Since 1960, Nigeria, Gabon and Angola have blossomed into major exporters and other significant producers include the Republic of the Congo, Cameroon, Zaire, the Ivory Coast and Sudan. In the future the last two should join the privileged ranks of the net exporters. Yet exploration of likely sources – in the West African coast and East Africa – is still only in its infancy.

Other energy sources are plentiful in certain areas, but entail enormous retrieval costs. Large coal deposits exist in Botswana, Swaziland and Zimbabwe (currently Africa's major producer). Areas with major river systems offer good potential for hydroelectric power generation. Large power projects now operate at Kariba on the Zambia–Zimbabwe border, the Volta River in eastern Ghana and Cabora Bassa in Mozambique. However, only when linked with power-intensive electrometallurgical industries such as aluminium, or with electrochemical industries does the requisite investment of hundreds of millions of dollars become economically feasible. Thus, Zaire, Madagascar, Cameroon, Tanzania, Gabon, Niger, and the Sudan cannot easily capitalize on their major river systems.[4]

It is true that a small number of African countries are mineral-rich. But the wealth of Africa is not as abundant in this respect as is often thought. Consider that South Africa alone mines the bulk of Africa's gold and diamonds. A number of other countries also export these precious metals or such strategic minerals as uranium, cobalt, chromite, vanadium or such crucial industrial raw materials as copper, bauxite, manganese, iron ore and tin.[5] Especially vital energy and mineral producers include Nigeria, Gabon, Zaire, Zambia, Zimbabwe and Botswana. But the stark reality is that the majority of African countries boast no important deposits, or, as of now, these riches are undiscovered. The giant mineral corporations have, furthermore, spent increasingly less on African exploration in response to unstable political conditions.

Moreover, Zaire, described by some as Africa's *el dorado*, instructs us that an abundance of resources is no guarantee of rapid development. A leading world producer of copper, cobalt, industrial diamonds and coffee, it also boasts gold, zinc and tin, immense timber reserves and considerable promise as an exporter of palm oil, rubber, cotton and tea. Ample sources of hydroelectric power and plenty of arable land complete this rosy portrait. But Zaire's economic record is dismal. An inflation rate of about 100 per cent and an enormous foreign debt (approximately US $6 billion in 1983) suggest the extent of failure. Industrial and agricultural production are in decline, public services continue to deteriorate and a chronic shortage of consumer goods combine to plague the people.

Why this lost promise? After all, the Ivory Coast, Kenya, and Malawi have done well in terms of growth rates in the sixties and seventies and have done so without significant natural resources. The key apparently lies in the area of public management – or rather, the degree of mismanagement, an issue considered in Chapter 6.

Small local markets are also a real hindrance to African economic development. About a third of the countries under discussion have less than two million inhabitants. Two-thirds have less than 10 million (Table 2). Some are equivalent in size to small cities; Cape Verde, Comoros, Equatorial Guinea, São Tome and Principe and Seychelles all count under 500,000. Only Zaire (29 million), Ethiopia (32 million) and Nigeria (80 million) contain reasonably large domestic markets. Thus, part of Africa's problem is clearly definable; its countries are burdened with the worst of all possible worlds – population pressure on the very limited arable land and a small (in numbers and income per capita) total market. The effective demand of an African country of five million people is, according to the Economic Commission for Africa, about equal to that of an American city of 100,000.

Clearly, economic associations or common markets are needed to mitigate the problem of small market size. Since the mid-seventies, there have been several attempts to promote monetary and trade cooperation: the Economic Community of West African States in 1975 (16 member countries, including Nigeria), the Southern African Development Coordination Conference in 1980 (nine member countries), the Preferential Trade Area in 1981 (nine countries in East and Central Africa, but stillborn until late 1983) and the Central African Economic Community in 1983 (10 French- and Portuguese-speaking countries). The goal of all this activity was voiced at the 1980 Organization of African Unity's Special Economic Summit – an All African Common Market by the year 2000. But this road will be a long and precarious one. The splintering of the East African

Table 2. *Population of subsaharan African countries, 1980*

Population (millions)	Number of countries (total = 45)
< 2	16
2–10	20
10–20	6
> 20	3

Source: computed from C. Cook, and D. Killingray, *African Political Facts Since 1945* (New York: Facts on File, 1983), 201–20.

Community in February 1977 dramatized the danger that rivalries and suspicions of unfair advantage will get out of hand. Intra-African trade expansion is crucial to Africa's industrialization, but the process is fraught with difficulties.

Raw economic potential is also limited by the availability of managerial and technical skills. In Africa, the demand for trained administrators and technicians is large, partly because governments intervene extensively in economic life. Typically, statutory boards and public corporations regulate economic activities, provide services and participate in production and/or distribution. But the supply of skilled indigenous manpower is meagre. At independence, according to the World Bank's *Accelerated Development in Subsaharan Africa* (1981), over three-quarters of the high-level manpower in government and private business were foreigners. At one extreme, Zaire had not a single African doctor, lawyer, or engineer in 1960. At the other extreme, Nigeria and Senegal were far better endowed. Still, Africans held only 700 of the 3,000 senior posts in the Nigerian civil service in 1955 and 1,500 Frenchmen still occupied most of the top Senegalese bureaucratic posts in 1961. This shortage of human resources continues today, exacerbated by the high world demand for these individuals and the decline in the quality of university education in numerous African countries because of underfunding and political interference.

Bitter ethnic and religious schisms are another internal constraint on capitalist development. Social tension and collective violence discourage investment, and worthy projects must be aborted. A culturally homogeneous population is a real boon for capitalist development; the governing elite is better able to motivate its people through patriotic appeals and foster nation-building solidarity, dedication and sacrifice. (Political schisms central to the understanding of the politics of capitalist development will be considered at length in Chapter 3.)

These, then, are the elements that determine raw economic potential. But this balance sheet is worthless on its own. The state must play an active role in exploiting its country's potential, in part by seeking a lucrative niche for the local economy within the world market system. The dimensions of this task can best be examined by focussing now on external constraints.

Does the international economy obstruct African capitalist development? This is a controversial issue. But less questionable is the proposition that international exchanges are inequitable in the sense that their benefits are unequally distributed. A bias against the poor countries handicaps accumulation there.

For Africa, the crucial period in the development of these inequities was the final third of the nineteenth century. In this epoch, several countries in Europe and North America vaulted ahead into sustained industrial growth. Simultaneously, Africa was being converted into colonies and protectorates by the industrializing countries. It is extremely doubtful whether Africa would have industrialized in the absence of imperialism. Yet the colonial powers did erect new barriers to industrialization as they structured their colonies' economies in a self-serving fashion. The benefits they obtained included secure sources of inexpensive raw materials and foodstuffs and markets for their manufactured goods. Colonial competition with metropolitan industry was discouraged until after World War II.[6]

The international division of labour was modified in the 1950s and 1960s as a belated though limited process of industrialization got underway in tropical Africa. Only a few colonies such as Senegal, Kenya, the Belgian Congo and Southern Rhodesia gained much manufacturing investment before the late fifties. These pioneers offered their foreign investors relatively large expatriate markets and advanced economic infrastructure.* It was not until independence that most colonies were able to progress much beyond the manufacture of beverages, food and cigarettes. Even thereafter, manufacturing investment typically extended only to some local processing of raw materials and local assembly or fabrication of formerly imported consumer goods (Table 3). Contemporary Africa continues to supply mainly primary products to the world market. Its flow of imports has somewhat altered; industrial economies now provide fewer manufactured consumer imports, concentrating instead on machinery, intermediate goods and locally unavailable raw materials. Of prime importance is the import of technology.

This pattern of exchange has presented considerable problems for capital accumulation* in Africa. Most obviously, African latecomers cannot exploit factors which facilitated the industrial revolution in Europe, Japan and the United States[7] – captive markets for industrial exports and raw material imports cheapened by slave labour or low

Table 3. *Distribution of Manufacturing by Industry in Continental Africa, 1971*

	Light Manufacturing[a] Industries		Heavy Manufacturing[b] Industries		Other Manufacturing Industries		Total Manufacturing	
	% output	no. persons engaged	% output	no. persons engaged	% output	no. persons engaged	%	no.
Egypt	74.9	439,910	24.9	211,360	0.2	2,280	100	653,550
Ghana	74.4	43,187	25.2	12,138	0.4	253	100	55,578
Ivory Coast	62.4	27,440	34.5	8,137	3.1	1,210	100	36,787
Nigeria	63.0	101,507	36.2	44,386	0.8	2,665	100	148,558
Senegal	76.7	11,510	23.3	3,150	0.0	—	100	14,660
Zaire	54.4	63,132	44.0	21,496	1.6	1,224	100	85,852
Kenya	57.2	38,615	41.6	35,171	1.2	1,312	100	75,098
Tanzania	73.8	41,103	24.2	6,729	2.0	866	100	48,698
Uganda	72.7	34,558	27.2	6,131	0.1	37	100	40,726
Zambia	63.1	30,998	36.7	17,707	0.2	239	100	48,944
Total Independent African countries	67.9	1,263,556	31.2	521,372	0.9	38,936	100	1,823,864

Notes:

a 'light manufacturing' includes food, beverages and tobacco; textiles and clothing; wood and furniture; and paper, printing and publishing.

b 'heavy manufacturing' includes chemicals, petroleum and plastics; non-metallic mineral products; basic metal industries; and fabricated metal products, machinery and equipment.

wages. In contrast, Africa must compete in world markets already dominated by technologically sophisticated transnational corporations.* Is this challenge surmountable? Yes, judging by the recent success of the Newly Industrializing Countries (NICs) in East Asia and Latin America. But the task is extremely complex and one calling for great ingenuity.

Beyond this, Africa's international economic exchanges tend to benefit disproportionately the developed partners. 'International trade', according to the Nobel prize winner, Gunnar Myrdal, 'will generally tend to breed inequality, and will do so the more strongly when substantial inequalities are already established.'[8] The disparity in economic power between the advanced capitalist countries and their African partners gives the latter no leverage in negotiating a better deal. Their influence is lessened by several factors. African markets are typically small, and therefore unattractive. Their specialization in one or a handful of exports means that their economies are vulnerable to fluctuations in world prices. When prices are low or natural disasters strike, they must turn to the West and the international institutions the West dominates for loans and aid. Finally, the concentration of research and development work in industrial countries means that Africa depends on transnational corporations for process and product technologies.* Vis-à-vis large, diversified and technologically complex industrial economies, Africa is in an extremely weak position.

This weakness is aptly demonstrated by the economic havoc wrought in Africa by the recent Western recession. 'Stagflation' in industrial countries both decreased world demand for (and hence unit value of) Africa's primary exports and increased the cost of this continent's manufactured imports. This, together with a second rapid escalation of oil prices in 1979, produced large balance-of-payments deficits for African oil importers. Exorbitant interest rates after 1980 exacerbated the problem. By 1982, the IMF was inundated with requests from its Third-World members, including those in Africa, for loans to rescue economies in which debt-servicing consumed a third or half of all foreign receipts. But the IMF did not have the resources equal to the task. All these factors helped move African economies into severe depression by 1983–4.

Of course, not all African countries are equally weak. Nigeria, in particular, is of considerable economic significance. It supplies 40 per cent of US oil imports, it is the largest single market in Africa for the industrial world, and it is Britain's leading export market outside the European Economic Community. Heavy Western investment in oil and manufacturing since 1970 has built a significant foreign stake in Nigeria's economy. But Nigeria's political weaknesses – corruption, divisions and disorganization – detract considerably from its impact on the international economy. Thus, international exchanges continue to favour powerful, well-organized countries.

What are the mechanisms that perpetuate these inequalities? Consider first international trade.[9] On the one hand, the prices that the transnational corporations charge their African customers for manufactured imports (consumer goods, intermediate products and machinery) are not mainly established by the laws of supply and demand in a free market. Increased costs can be passed on to consumers and productivity gains do not necessarily reduce proportionately the prices of products. On the other hand, the market does determine the world price of most of Africa's commodity exports. Therefore, higher production costs cannot necessarily be recouped. Also, a rise in productivity will lower world prices by increasing supply while demand remains fairly inelastic. This fundamental inequality, once established, is difficult to alter.

Various restrictive trade practices affect Africa's manufactured imports. First, oligopolies dominate most branches of manufacturing in Western countries. In the production of automobiles, electronics and drugs, for example, a handful of companies in each country account for the bulk of the output. Their position is virtually unassailable because of the major barriers to the entry of new firms. To equip themselves, undertake the requisite research activities and build consumer loyalty through advertising, aspirants need impossibly large financial and technical resources. Consequently, oligopolies are able to set their prices, not according to market forces, but their pricing policy. Competition takes the form mainly of the differentiation of a product from its rivals and of marketing strategies, not of price-cutting. In addition, at least one-third of international trade involves exchanges among different branches of the same vertically integrated firms. These exchanges are almost totally insulated from the play of market forces.

Primary producers in Africa have tried to create their own cartels to reduce competition and boost prices, but without much success. True, the large oil exporters in OPEC succeeded in forcing up oil prices in the 1970s. But such unusual conditions as the high world demand for oil and the small number of exporters aided their cause. If even OPEC cannot maintain a common front on quotas and prices in the 1980s, how much harder is it for the many producers of coffee, tea, cocoa, sugar, tin, bauxite and even copper to reach agreement?[10] Despairing of forming functioning producer cartels, African and other Third World governments have recently attempted to negotiate commodity stabilization agreements with Western governments. The idea is simple. An international authority stabilizes the world price for a particular commodity by establishing export quotas for members, stockpiling the commodity when world supplies are plentiful and selling only when demand outstrips new production. But the five international commodity agreements negotiated since 1976 (sugar in 1977, rubber in 1979, cocoa in 1980, tin in 1981 and coffee in 1983) have not been particularly effective in preventing wide price swings. The International Coffee Council was the most successful, building on its long experience in establishing export quotas for member countries.

Not only does there continue to be wild oscillations in the world price for Africa's commodities, but the trend since the 1960s is downwards in both the terms of trade and the purchasing power of non-oil exports (Table 4). Cocoa, coffee, tea, cotton, sugar, copper, iron ore, phosphates, all brought depressed world prices in 1982. The weighted average price index of primary commodities had fallen 26.7 per cent during 1981 and 1982, according to IMF data. Whereas 100 units of phosphates purchased 100 units of manufactured goods in 1975, by 1982 the same quantity of manufactured imports required 205 units of phosphates. The squeeze this sort of decline in purchasing power placed on the foreign exchange position of African governments requires no elaboration. Although most commodity prices rallied in 1983, the recovery was shortlived. Prices began to fall again in 1984.

Another factor which works against the economic interests of Africa is the tendency for much of the processing of primary products to be done in developed countries. Governments of industrialized countries obviously want to reap the local employment and profit benefits which such processing entails. Their cascading tariffs, that is tariffs which rise with each stage of processing, encourage transnationals to import primary commodities in their rawest feasible state. Third World countries are thereby deprived of the industrial impetus that local processing of their exports could provide.

The disparity between industrial and African countries is

Table 4. *Terms of trade of low-income developing countries*
(1978 = 100)

	Change in terms of trade (%)[a]		Change in purchasing power of exports (%)[b]	
	1973–6	1979–82	1973–6	1978–82
Asia	12.1	− 3.2	58.5	15.7
Africa	− 15.3	− 13.8	− 18.7	− 3.5

Notes:
a   ratio of export unit value index over import unit value index.
b   product of terms of trade and export quantum index.
Source: World Bank, *World Development Report*, 1983, Table 2.4

further exacerbated by the global location of research and development. About 98 per cent of these activities occur in the North, especially in the US, Western Europe and Japan, according to the Brandt Commission's famous 1980 *Report of the Independent Commission on International Issues.* More advanced research facilities and generous salaries in the industrial countries encourage the migration of scientific personnel from the South to the North. And the immigration rules in developed countries encourage this movement, while strictly controlling the inflow of unskilled labour. Without many of its most innovative scientists and technicians, Africa grows weaker in a world which highly values technological prowess.

Despite these international economic practices, we are not suggesting that the international economic order is an insurmountable obstacle to development. Some simplistic neo-Marxist dependency theorists have advanced this notion which has gained wide currency in Africa. In Tanzania, for example, teachers and students in even the most remote one-room schoolhouse can recite an impressive litany of imperialism's depredations. Leading figures in *Chama Cha Mapinduzi*, Tanzania's governing party, and the government also apparently embrace this comforting notion which absolves them of blame for the current economic catastrophe. But delusions are always poor policy guidelines, no matter how psychologically satisfying. By inflating special challenges and inequities into an immutable constraint, Tanzanians (and others) hurt only themselves; such thinking impedes creative and constructive responses to the current crisis.

Certain governments, unblinded by such ideological constraints, have ably exploited the limited opportunities available in the international division of labour. The Ivory Coast, a small West African nation of 8.5 million, has enjoyed considerable economic growth by means of economic dependency. In 1950, the Ivorian manufacturing sector was minuscule – two small canneries, a few soap factories, a spinning mill, a sawmill and a couple of factories for beer and mineral water. Thirty years later they boasted a diversified manufacturing sector of 705 enterprises; their turnover in 1980 was about 650 billion francs CFA (US \$3.1 billion) with about one-third aimed at export markets. Internal linkages among industries and economic sectors flourished. Although in 1980 chemicals, building materials and electronics still had to import their manufacturing materials, other industries could rely upon local sources. The agricultural sector was able to provide more than half these local inputs. Thus, industrialization proceeded apace with agricultural diversification. Healthy agro-industries sprung up in textiles, palm oil and fruit processing, much of the output destined for export.[11]

What was the blueprint for this success? Essentially, the plan was built around extracting whatever benefits the existing economic order could offer. In its 1978 report,

Ivory Coast: The Challenge of Success, the World Bank claimed that the government in the sixties:

was fully aware that further economic success was dependent on more foreign capital and labour. Political and economic stability and growth, together with a liberal policy toward foreign investors, were considered essential in creating the confidence abroad needed to acquire these production factors. [...] Given the outward-oriented policy chosen by the Ivory Coast, it was important to preserve and cultivate close economic and political relations with France and the Francophone neighbors. The country needed the former for capital, expertise, skilled labor, and markets, and the latter for both unskilled labor and markets. (p. 16)

That is, the Ivorian strategy was to industrialize and revolutionize agriculture by maintaining a neocolonial orientation to France and exploiting migrant labour from the poverty stricken neighbouring countries, especially Bourkina Fasso and Mali. The costs entailed were considerable – not only to the alien Africans who comprise about half the Ivorian labour force, but also to the Ivorian national pride. Whether the capitalist development achieved was justifiable is a matter of judgment. Clearly, though, many have benefitted, including the desperate migrant labourers who would have been even worse off without the Ivorian 'miracle'.

Leaving aside the moral issue, one point is clear: consistent and shrewd policy can mitigate the inequalities of the world economy or even capitalize on them. But this requires a strong state*. It is to the crucial question of the state that we now turn.

Increasing state power and capitalist expansion have long been intimately linked. In Western Europe, the modern state was born precisely during the Industrial Revolution. State-building, the creation of a centralized and hierarchical system of authority relations within a certain territory, required that local political units be subordinated to the

central government. To achieve this, ambitious rulers inces-
santly strove for new revenues to fuel the expansion of
standing armies and administrative staffs. This search, in
turn, contributed to the broadening of capitalist property
relations and the incorporation of backward regions into
national markets. On the one hand, as commerce and
industry grew so did the state's tax base. On the other hand,
this increased money supply put the ruler in a position to
boost economic growth by government enforcement of
national legal codes and tariffs, building infrastructure and
extending the state's sway abroad.[12]

And what of the myth of *laissez-faire*? As a policy, it has
always been just that – more myth than practice. Even in
nineteenth-century Britain where private enterprise played
a much stronger role than elsewhere, this was true. Britain
was unique in that class struggles had produced a robust and
politically influential bourgeoisie as early as the eighteenth
century. But even here the state had to create the prerequi-
site institutional conditions for capitalist development. The
framework of political stability, social harmony and administrative centralization, born of the civil strife of the seventeenth century, allowed market forces to operate efficiently.
Security of property and life, predictability in administration, a compact and unified national market and a protected
international trade all gave impetus to the capitalist
impulse.[13]

On the Continent, industrialization was fostered by vig-
orous state interference. First, institutional obstacles to
economic expansion associated with the *ancien régime* had
to be eradicated. Central governments abolished feudal
land tenure, the feudal labour control system and the
autonomous taxation powers of local authorities. Legal
systems that failed to safeguard private property or security
of contract, and distorted and inequitable tax regulations
were altered. Along with the maintenance of social order

and labour discipline, these actions fostered a fertile setting for capitalist relations.

Then too, the state played a more direct role. It undertook to build and maintain certain necessary but unprofitable services such as education, technical training, electricity and transport systems, roads and communications. Governments also became directly involved in production. Steel, for example, was essential to the diversification of an industrial base, but sometimes too risky an investment to interest private investors. To encourage both capital and entrepreneurship in such key areas, governments offered various baits – tariff protection, tax write-offs and subsidies or even public participation in industries.[14]

In countries late to industrialize, the state has played an even more vital role. In Japan, the Meiji Government confronted in the mid nineteenth century the challenge of foreign penetration. Upon deciding that Japanese autonomy could only be retained by increased military strength and that this would necessitate the modernization of society and economy, it zealously set about this mammoth task. The 'revolution from above' included: dissolving the communal village economy by enclosure and the institution of private property; freeing the serfs, thus establishing a labour market; settling peasants on their own land; instituting free primary education; building the basic economic infrastructure; and providing credit to industrialists. The Japanese, therefore, met the foreign challenge by constructing a diversified industrial economy and a powerful military machine. There was a price, of course – fascism, imperialism, and eventually even the agonies of the Second World War.[15]

How can one account for the success of the Japanese which others, for example the Chinese, were unable to duplicate? Certainly, Japan has not been blessed with an abundance of natural resources; the country has little coal, iron or oil. Also unpropitious was the domination of foreign markets by the early industrializers. One explanation offered is attitudinal – that the Japanese sense of diligence, thrift and responsibility was conducive to economic growth. Whatever the validity of this position, another factor was clearly crucial: the unusual capacity of the state to implement an ambitious reform programme. A public bureaucracy highly responsive to business concerns and with marked elan and competence emerged. But just as vital was the broad public support that the state's programme commanded. Diverse classes and strata, the bourgeoisie, aristocracy and military leaders, were unified by an appeal to patriotism, the notion that the economy was meant to serve the interests of national power and glory rather than the individual. This heady notion, which also contained the seeds of fascism,[16] helps explain the docility of the working class as well.

The state also figures dramatically in explanations of the contemporary economic success of the Newly Industrializing Countries of East Asia – Taiwan, South Korea, Hong Kong and Singapore. They combine shrewd policy choices with an advanced implementational capacity. Consider the case of Taiwan. The Guomindang government, since the early 1950s, has promoted an agricultural revolution and rapid industrialization. Land reform in 1953 required landlords to sell all their holdings which exceeded a specified ceiling to their tenants and workers. The state then extracted a reasonable surplus from smallholders through its monopoly of fertilizer distribution as well as pricing policy and taxes. These fiscal resources were used to promote agricultural productivity and subsidize urban industry. The groundwork for rapid industrialization was superbly laid: political stability, guarantees to foreign investors, the availability to industrialists of public credits and direct participation of public corporations in industries with significant externalities,* all advanced the cause. And tariff policy plus incentives to exports have directed this industrial growth towards foreign markets.[17]

Special conditions apparently account for Taiwan's situation. As Japan did, Taiwan confronts an external threat – China's determination to repossess it. Fortified with this threat, the government implemented a programme of significant reform; at one and the same time it was clever enough to eradicate the most glaring rural inequities that could fuel an insurrection and to augment agricultural productivity. The Guomindang has also ably appealed to patriotism to rally support for its policies from business and other sectors. Here, too, economic growth is couched in terms of building state power and the capacity to resist the communist threat.

In sum, the state has everywhere facilitated capitalist accumulation. The phenomenon is universal. Africa can be no exception. The public sector is central to Africa's economic development; who will sponsor industrialization if not the state? There is no local business class which dominates industry. Some agency – and that is the state – must find a niche for the local economy in the highly competitive global market discussed above. And a priority on local accumulation must be enforced. Only the state can fulfil this role.

Specifically, the exigencies of contemporary capitalism require the state to create and maintain a number of conditions. First and most fundamental, the general socio-political and legal framework must be conducive to market relationships. An environment of security of property and predictability is basic to encourage investment; in turn, this requires political stability and a minimum degree of social harmony. Otherwise, capitalists cannot calculate that an investment today will bear fruit tomorrow. A legal code that protects the prerogatives of the owners and is officially respected (and hence calculable) is another element. Such a code must, of course, create and protect a unified national market by limiting or eliminating the taxation power of local authorities. And it should foster a stable and rational taxation system that encourages investment. Also vital is the protection of the institution of private property through such steps as: limiting the claims of employees, abolishing traditional land tenure, safeguarding the sanctity of contracts, and guaranteeing full compensation in the event of nationalization.

Second, a range of economic conditions must be fostered by the state. Services that directly facilitate production – roads, railways, ports, airports, electricity, water and telecommunications – is one of these. Essential public services that indirectly assist production as they promote a skilled, healthy, motivated labour force are also important; these include schools, technical education, public housing, sanitation and facilities for sports and health. The public sector may also intervene directly through subsidy or investment in industries which are essential to expansion of complementary industries but are too risky to attract private investors. Publicly owned steel or transport or cement may sometimes play a significant economic role even if they are not profitable in themselves.

Finally, the state should regulate foreign economic relations in order to maximize the local benefits. This is a most delicate task. On the one hand, the government is striving to attract foreign investment to particular industries and negotiate favourable trading arrangements with industrial countries. If the conditions sketched above are met, transnationals will probably be drawn to invest – provided some local economic potential exists. On the other hand, the local state must defend the national interest in the local accumulation of capital, foreign exchange, employment and expertise. This will require, at the minimum, some regulation of

e transnationals' economic activities, for otherwise the
tter's global profit considerations will jeopardize the
:hievement of local economic priorities. To both attract
ıd regulate foreign investment – this is the challenge
ɔnfronting public officials who wish to push capitalist
evelopment in the context of the existing world economy.

Capitalist development thus places enormously complex
emands on political systems. (Socialist development is
ıore exacting still.) In response, today's state or public
·ctor extends far beyond the familiar three branches of
ɔvernment, executive, legislative and judicial, even in
beral democracies. The African state also embraces the
ıstruments of legitimate coercion (military and police),
·gulatory agencies, parastatals,* regional and/or local gov-
·nment and administration, the social services (hospitals,
:hools and transport companies), the government-con-
olled mass media and trade-union apparatus and the
ɔverning party (its identity often merging with that of the
ɔvernment). Such a heterogeneous collection of organiza-
ɔns is not easily steered down a common course.

Neither consistency nor efficiency characterize the public
·ctor of most African countries. In fact, most regimes
·tively *discourage* the mobilization and productive invest-
ıent of resources. Only a small minority of African states
·tains an effective directive capacity.

At one extreme of this spectrum are the 'fictitious
ates'.[18] These states exist in the minimal sense that other
ɔvernments recognize a regime's claim to territorial sover-
gnty. But they fail to comply with the Weberian definition
f a modern state – a hierarchical system of authority
·lations ultimately maintained by a monopoly of legiti-
ıate coercion. Instead, such countries as Chad, Uganda,
quatorial Guinea and Zaire are 'run' by warlords or
roups of armed men without the benefit of functioning
ate structures. In these countries, it is misleading to talk of

a developmental orientation or strategy; the aim of mo
public officials (except during periodic clean-up campaign
is simply personal aggrandizement. Weaker states a·
usually clients of the major powers. Transnational corpor:
tions exploit opportunities for superscale profits, in co·
laboration with the local political elite. Foreign gover·
ments, especially the French, Belgian, American an·
Libyan, act as external protectors of friendly regimes f·
strategic and/or economic reasons. Meanwhile, the con
mon people and their concerns receive short shrift.

At the far end of the spectrum is a mere handful of health
states; the Ivory Coast, Cameroon, Kenya, Malawi, M·
zambique and Senegal are highly structured and capable ·
devising and implementing diverse policies. However, in th
African context, the designation 'healthy' is relative. A
tempted *coups*, localized insurrection and bureaucratic co
ruption are not strangers in even these countries. The·
governments cannot always overcome resistance to unpo·
ular edicts by peripheral communities. Nonetheless, eac
has executed programmes of social change and a few ha·
shown themselves adept at coming to terms with the inte·
national economy.

But what of the majority of African states? They fa·
between the two poles, although today it must be said th:
most more closely resemble the fictitious states. How ca·
one account for this widespread political failure? And wha·
specifically, are the manifestations of this failure? It is t·
these issues that we now turn – to political decay an·
economic crisis, the central concerns of this book.

Africa's economic and social problems derive in part fro·
inappropriate policy. In agriculturally dependent econ·
mies, the state's primary concern should be to safeguard an·
expand agricultural production. Yet just the opposite effe·
is created by certain policies. Price controls on foodstuff·

w producer prices for agricultural exports, overvalued
irrencies and high protective tariffs on manufactures turn
ie rural–urban terms of trade decisively against agri-
iltural producers. Tax revenues, drawn disproportionate-
from the primary sector, are allocated disproportionately
the urban areas in the form of subsidized public credit to
ommerce and industry and public investment. The results
re negative: the production of foodstuffs and cash crops is
iscouraged and a massive rural exodus to the cities is
imulated. Together, agricultural stagnation or decline
nd urban growth escalate black-market food prices and
estrict foreign exchange and state revenues.

Deeper probing reveals that the state's failure lies as
iuch at the level of policy implementation as formulation.
ew government leaders are unaware of the need for poli-
es to stimulate agricultural production. African politi-
ans know farmers will produce only if they are promptly
nd adequately compensated and if they believe their goods
in and will be marketed. Year after year governments offer
olemn promises – agriculture is declared to have top
riority. But the same problems persist: low producer
rices, delays in payment and deteriorating market organi-
ition and infrastructure. In practice, reform laws are
nored. Hence, the credibility of the government sinks even
irther.

This pattern is emerging even in countries which were
elatively efficient agricultural producers in the sixties and
eventies. Consider Kenya. 'For several years', one frus-
ated critic wrote in 1983, 'policies have been outlined,
ften published and even elaborately launched, but have
iiled to be properly implemented.' The National Food
olicy (launched in Sessional Paper No. 4 in 1980), for
istance, fully accords with current thinking that agri-
iltural productivity must be motivated through material
icentives. In practice, however, maize and wheat farmers

have been forced into long waits before they are compensat
ed by inefficient and corrupt marketing boards. Conse
quently, the inevitable happened; production of these com
modities fell in the eighties while imports rose. 'Clearly th
central issue revolves around how to reverse the govern
ment management slide, because no amount of policy state
ments or promises of improved efficiency will make any rea
difference until this is done.'[19]

Agriculture is one important case. But more fundamen
tally, public sectors are incapable of maintaining most o
the conditions which foster economic growth; they ar
overwhelmed by their own incoherence, indiscipline an
shrinking fiscal base. Potential investors – both foreign an
indigenous – are not willing to gamble on a climate o
political instability, political violence and unequal applica
tions of the law. A rational and predictable administratio
encourages capitalist accumulation, but public mismanage
ment which grows out of systemic corruption, incompe
tence and demoralization are all negatives. Essentia
services deteriorate. Public corporations operate at a los
Inequities and inconsistencies in tax administration encour
age fraud and vitiate sound fiscal policy. Public official
seem unwilling or unable to create the delicate balanc
between attracting and squeezing foreign investors. Th
stage is set for the aborting of capitalist development.

Why is this pattern the common one in postcoloni?
Africa? In the succeeding two chapters we will show ho\
political weaknesses are rooted in particular historical an
social conditions. In Africa, the relationship between stat
and society differs markedly from that in the early stages o
capitalist development in the West or Japan. The moder
state in these latter countries evolved within a context o
class societies. In Britain, France and the United States, a
ascendant bourgeoisie managed to establish its hegemony
In Germany and Japan, capitalist transformation wa

pressed through the state by an aristocracy determined to modernize the economy and build national power through a 'revolution from above'.[20] The governmental apparatus in all these cases was very unlikely to act against the long-run interests of the dominant class. Also, state institutions commanded a considerable measure of consent from all social classes. Cultural homogenization permitted appeals to patriotism or nationalism to override sectional interests with a vision of national goals. In the twentieth century, the distributive capacity of the welfare state and the legitimacy accorded democratic rules and procedures fortified popular consent. In sum, the Western state today is disciplined and responsive because of the demands of class power and a pluralist political system. The state's power is enhanced by a general willingness amongst the citizenry to comply with governmental directives. The result is a relatively strong governmental organization.

The African situation is enormously different. Peasants – the majority of the population – are only marginally involved in the national market and political life. An indigenous business class in its embryonic stages of development is highly dependent on the state. Although foreign capital is important, its political power is reduced by its divided national origin and imperialist associations. There is no strong landed aristocracy to spearhead a revolution from above. Where then is the social agent to champion capitalist transformation? Coupled with this lack is the general sense that the state is an alien body; it was imposed upon a disparate society by European imperialists. A nation is really non-existent in most cases, nor may it even be in the process of formation. Class forces are weak, but communal ties flourish. This is the result of primordial identities extended and intensified by uneven development and group competition in the new territorial arenas. Ethnic conflict raises the costs of state making; the loyalty of the subject population is in doubt. Patriotism in these circumstances is of limited use as a mobilizing ideology.

Personal rule, a form of patrimonialism, is the best-adapted system of governance to these conditions. Unable to depend on the willing compliance of bureaucrats and citizens, rulers turn to mercenary incentives and force. The typical scenario goes something like this: a strongman emerges; his rule is based on managing a complex system of patron–client linkages and factional alliances; and he maintains a personally loyal armed force to support him at every turn.

Personal rule can be dangerous, though. Inherent in this system is the likelihood that no one harbours the will or capacity to keep in check its destructive features. The cynical tactics of political support-building and self-enrichment undermine the state's already fragile authority and demoralize even the most honest and loyal public officials. One of many African writers who laments this condition is Chinua Achebe. The narrator of *A Man of the People* expresses this disenchantment:

> They [the villagers] were not only ignorant but cynical. Tell them that this man [the Minister] had used his position to enrich himself and they would ask you – as my father did – if you thought that a sensible man would spit out the juicy morsel that good fortune placed in his mouth. (p. 2)

The omnipresent danger is political decay – a decline in the political and administrative institutions of the state shown through the prevalence of political violence and instability and bureaucratic incompetence and corruption.[21] Like a disease, political decay attacks the well-being of the people. The economy will not attract investors who are naturally frightened of violence, instability and arbitrary administration. A political logic of survival dictates the allocation of public jobs and resources, but this is totally irrational from the viewpoint of capital accumulation. In sum, the state cannot maintain the essential conditions for a thriving capitalism.

A self-reinforcing downward spiral of political decay and economic deterioration is the principal danger. Once underway, this pattern gathers steam and is difficult to reverse. Political violence and bureaucratic ineptitude lay waste to the modern economy. *Pari passu*, a parallel economy or black market flourishes outside state control. This, in turn, feeds on bureaucratic corruption and the avoidance of regulations and taxes. The state is undermined further by the erosion of public revenues and the ineffectiveness of the civil service.

At the nadir of this spiral lies chaos. A fictitious state of armed men detaches itself from society and preys upon a dying economy. This picture is a grim one, but not as we will show, without hope.

§ 3 §

COLONIAL ROOTS OF THE CONTEMPORARY CRISIS

Some of Africa's problems are rooted in the colonial experience. The imperial powers failed in various ways to erect a sturdy base for responsive and effective postcolonial states.

In the first place, the territories created by imperialism were, in a dual sense, artificial entities, and this has produced severe problems in state building. First, their political forms at independence had not evolved organically out of local traditions. Instead, colonial powers transferred Western models of state organization to Africa. These imports might have taken root in local political cultures, given an extended germination period. However, colonialism was an almost fleeting experience in most of Africa, too transitory to institutionalize alien political structures and norms. Secondly, the colonies and protectorates were artificial in the sense that late nineteenth-century European imperialists paid no heed to cultural and linguistic criteria in carving out national boundaries. Diverse and sometimes hostile peoples were grouped within common borders. These differences were exacerbated, albeit unintentionally, by colonial-induced social, economic and political change. The legitimacy crisis and ethnic tensions that bedevil postcolonial politics must be understood in the context of the colonial epoch.

In the second place, colonial capitalism was not a particularly dynamic or creative force; this, too, has implications for the contemporary period. Imperialism dragged, prodded and enticed Africans into a market economy, but most participated only marginally. Economic change there was, and along with this, the formation of modern capitalist classes. A small bourgeoisie and proletariat of sorts appeared upon the historical stage. But outside the towns the capitalist impulse floundered. Agriculture was largely the province of smallholders whose operations were only partly affected by market conditions. In settler colonies like Kenya and Southern Rhodesia, markets in land, labour and commodities held wider sway; even here, though, modern capitalist class formation was in its embryonic stage. What emerged from the colonial experience more closely resembled peasant societies than capitalist ones – and furthermore peasant societies without a politically and economically dominant class. Class was not the key to unlock the secrets of all political struggles; ethnicity was to figure centrally. The economically fragile emergent bourgeoisie was unable to enforce its capitalist priorities on the state apparatus.

Patrimonialism was the political adaptation to these social and economic realities. Unpropitious conditions were to shade this mode of governance with a particularly personalistic and oppressive cast.

Consider first the external origins of African political institutions. State structures are most likely to win popular support if they evolve organically rather than being imposed from outside. In Africa, however, there was rarely any organic link between the political institutions prescribed in constitutions and the indigenous institutions of the precolonial period.

States, in the sense of centralized authorities able to impose their will in a territory via an administrative, judicial and coercive apparatus, did emerge in precolonial Africa, especially in the North and the West.[1] An economic surplus is one necessary condition for the formation of a state, permitting the support of an urban-based ruling class and governing institutions. In Africa, states were financed either through a settled and prosperous agriculture, the proceeds of plunder (usually in the form of slaves or cattle), and/or the revenues deriving from long-distance trade. Rulers imposed tribute on subjects – cash, grain, precious metals, ivory or slaves – and taxes on imports and exports. Kings and chiefs, in return, provided internal order, defence, the protection and regulation of the land, the construction of public works and important ritual functions such as rain-making. The absence of a written language (outside the spheres of Egyptian and Arab influence) was the greatest impediment to the formation of strong states; record-keeping is essential to efficient administration.

Nonetheless, many kingdoms waxed and waned in precolonial Africa. Given a different set of historical circumstances, some of them might have formed the building blocks for contemporary nation-states. The great medieval savanna kingdoms of Western Africa such as Ghana, Mali and Songhai successively rose and declined before the imposition of colonial rule. Of especially rich tradition were the ancient kingdoms of the Nubians in Kush on the Nile and the Ethiopians in Axum. And more recent were the kingdom of Buganda, founded in the seventeenth century in what is now Southern Uganda, and the Lozi Kingdom of Barotseland, now Zambia, established only in the early nineteenth century. In the dark tropical forest area of West Africa, powerful and prosperous states like Asante (present day Ghana) and Benin (Eastern Nigeria) were born not so long ago. However, they were the exception to the general rule of small, isolated, egalitarian settlements in this region. All these states drew their revenues primarily from settled agriculture and pastoralism, though taxes on trade or slaving were also important in some cases.

Other states relied mainly on plunder. The Zulus, through the military genius of Dingiswayo and Shaka, created an empire in South Africa about the end of the eighteenth century. Cattle were the major form of tribute exacted from subjects. And Asante, Dahomey, the Yoruba states (all in West Africa) and Buganda were funded by the Atlantic and Arab slave trades.

Revenues from trade were especially significant to the Hausa states (presently in northern Nigeria) which participated in long distance exchanges with the Arabs across the Sahara. The Fulani conquered and united these states in the early nineteenth century, establishing their capital in Sokoto.

Alongside these empires, confederacies and unitary states were radically different societies. Often termed stateless or acephalous (headless) societies, these small, autonomous communities of cultivators or pastoralists were scattered throughout Africa. Societies lacking hierarchical political structures included the Ewe of eastern Ghana, the Ibo of eastern Nigeria, the Nuer and Dinka of southern Sudan and the Nilotic and Nilo-Hamitic peoples of Uganda, Kenya and Tanzania. All these peoples lacked a sense of common identity even though they spoke the same or mutually intelligible languages. The effective political unit was the village or kin-group. Disputes between these units were settled by negotiations and compromise, or by intergroup violence when negotiations failed and feelings ran high.

Africa thus evolved a variety of traditional political structures. But most of the countries created by colonialism contained several traditional societies, each of which valued its own political traditions, myths and symbols. This complicated state-building, since it was impossible to draw upon a single, traditional model in devising the modern state's institutions. A government's decision to adopt the indigenous political institutions and traditions of one community would be a virtual declaration of war against the excluded groups.

Nigeria aptly illustrates the diversity of political traditions that most contemporary African governments have inherited. Each of Nigeria's three major peoples embraced a distinct form of political organization.

In the north, the seven Hausa–Fulani emirates were among the most centralized, hierarchical and rigidly stratified kingdoms in tropical Africa. The Muslim Fulani established dominion over the indigenous Hausa following the *jihad* (holy war) of the early nineteenth century. The head or *emir* appointed his administrators. Various officials assisted him – a chief minister (*waziri*), the minister responsible for the judiciary (*alkali*), the minister of internal security (*dogari*) and advisers versed in Koranic law (the *mallamis*). Land and cattle taxes and tribute paid by subordinate chiefs supported the elaborate administrative structure and army. A patrimonial form with quasi-feudal characteristics, this system was, at least in principle, adaptable to modern bureaucratic organization.

The Yoruba, Nigeria's second most numerous people, operated a number of confederate political systems. Among the Oyo Yoruba, for instance, the *alafin* of Oyo headed several cleverly organized, semi-autonomous chiefdoms. A chief minister (*bashorun*), a prince (*aremo*) and two councils of chiefs (the *oyo mesi* and *ilari*) assisted him. The chiefly councils exercised considerable power over the *alafin*'s decisions. According to local custom, tributary chiefs emerged from local illustrious families and ruled at the provincial and district levels. The tax system, dependent largely on tribute, was not as complex as that of the emirates.

The Ibo, the third major ethnic group, lived largely within localized, acephalous communities. Only in a few towns such as Onitsha and Oguta in what is now eastern Nigeria was there a differentiated political system. Stateless in the sense that they had no central authority, these rural communities operated according to complex rules. The *eze* or *okpara-ukwu*, the most senior or highly respected elder, played the role of first among equals in the council of elders. Although certain decisions were taken by assemblies of all adult males in the villages, the council was the most influential element in decision-making. Lineage segments composed of those who traced their descent from a common ancestor constituted the framework of this complex political system. But age sets and occupational groups also made political demands, for example, for the construction or maintenance of markets or civic centres. Autonomous Ibo communities settled their differences by negotiation or violence, as there was no superior authority to whom they might appeal.

A difficult challenge faces African states which have not evolved out of a single dominant society. Their postcolonial rulers cannot fall back upon the legitimizing force of traditional institutions; the difference in scale and organization of the modern state is too significant. This is not to say that traditional imagery is shunned. Several independent countries adopted names which evoke the magic and glory of past African civilizations – Ghana, Mali, Benin, Zimbabwe – though these original societies had a tenuous or non-existent geographical link to the contemporary state. Rulers also attempt to buttress their authority through manipulation of time-honoured authority symbols, but these efforts are of doubtful success (see Chapter 5). The only common political tradition is often the colonial one and this is bureaucratic-authoritarian in nature.

Tradition is more politically relevant in those few precolonial countries where polities survived the colonial era intact. These number only five in tropical Africa: Ethiopia, Lesotho, Swaziland, Rwanda and Burundi. Quasi-feudal Ethiopia lasted until the ousting of Emperor Haile Selassie I and his court in 1974. In Rwanda, the quasi-feudal Tutsi aristocracy was displaced by the Hutu majority during the ethnic violence preceding its independence in 1962. Traditional political elements survive only in Lesotho, Swaziland and Burundi.

Consider the case of Swaziland, a small country bordered on three sides by the Republic of South Africa. Sobhuza II reigned over the Swazis for over 60 years until his death in August 1982. A colourful figure, Sobhuza, in 1973 suspended his country's Westminster-style constitution; just five years after independence, he reverted to the familiar rule of the benevolent autocrat. He retained a modern cabinet system and bureaucracy and even a personally selected parliament elected according to a unique indirect system to rubber-stamp his decisions. A handful of traditional advisory councils and roles were instituted. In the event of the king's death, the queen mother (*indlovukati*) was to assume power on an interim basis. The monarch was to be advised by three councils: *Libandla Laka Ngwane* (Council of the Swazi Nation), the *Libandla Ncane* (Standing Committee of the *Libandla*) and the *Liqoqo* (advisory council). The *Libandla*, which met regularly each year for about a month, is composed of all the chiefs and other notables chosen for their wisdom. The *Liqoqo*, on the other hand, is a more informal body with no fixed membership. This council was headed by the king's chief uncle and included a group of eminent princes, chiefs and selected commoners as *indvuna* (councillors) who could represent the king at royal functions. During Sobhuza's life, this convoluted system was quite effective and benign.

The death of the king in 1982 precipitated a power struggle within the ranks of the Swazi ruling house. Pretenders were encouraged to assert their claims by the absence of a constitution and modern political institutions. The principal contestants in the drama were Prime Minister Prince Mabandla, the Queen Regent Dzeliwe and the *Liqoqo*. By custom, the Queen Regent, one of Sobhuza's 50 widows, holds power until the coronation of a new king and his queen mother. But the *Liqoqo* flouted this accustomed course and tried to assert its primacy. And it was finally triumphant; by early 1984, a standing committee of the *Liqoqo* composed of four persons emerged as the real locus of power in Swaziland.

Tradition failed to provide an institutional mechanism for succession even in the case of Swaziland. What survives in that country is but a faint shadow of ancient political patterns. In more culturally heterogeneous societies, the challenge of adapting tradition to modern political needs is just that much more problematical. Rulers must, therefore, have recourse to foreign models of the state.

African countries are artifical, too, in the related sense that few of them constitute nation-states. A nation, on the one hand, is a social group that develops solidarity on the basis of shared customs and institutions; on the other hand, a state is a political organization laying claim to power in a particular territory.[2] Where nation and state are coterminous, ethnic loyalty (nationalism) fuses with state loyalty (patriotism). The state acquires legitimacy and internal cohesion permitting it to override personal and sectional preoccupations with a vision of a greater good. But in Africa the nation-state is a rarity. Although Swaziland, Lesotho and Somali qualify, the majority of African states are multinational (or poly-ethnic). This is a potentially debilitating feature of African political life; when citizens' loyalty extends no further than their own ethnic group, states are fragile indeed.

Not only did colonialism lump together heterogeneous peoples in common territories, it also, albeit unintentionally, sharpened ethnic consciousness.[3] Basing administrative boundaries and local government on cultural-linguistic lines as the colonial powers did fostered ethnicity. A divisive sense of separateness was promoted by the formation of local Native Authorities in British Africa to adminster land rights and certain taxes. The imperialists' assumption that Africans lived in tribes, and that these should therefore constitute the basis for administration, became a self-fulfilling perception.

A second important factor was the uneven regional impact of modernization as introduced by colonial rule. Some regions developed cash crops and prospered; others didn't. Railway construction spurred agricultural development in areas the line traversed. Towns, and hence urban employment, emerged in the homelands of certain groups, thus favouring their economic advance. The establishment of mission schools in certain regions, usually adjacent to the coast, gave local ethnic groups an enviable headstart with Western education. Consequently, some people benefitted from these opportunities for upward mobility, whereas others were regarded as backward. Uneven development thereby stimulated ethnic consciousness: those holding the advantage strove to retain it, whereas others clamoured for their fair share of the pie.

As independence approached, this dichotomous we–they mentality was underscored by a new fear – the suspicion on the part of the disadvantaged and/or peripheral people that the well-to-do tribes would consolidate their position by controlling the postcolonial state structure. Few politicians could resist the temptation to capitalize on these mutual anxieties to bolster their personal following. Politicians exploited, and thus magnified, ethnic consciousness by manipulating tribally-oriented cultural symbols and rhetoric which evoked tribal unity in the face of a common enemy. Aspiring leaders goaded their audience: 'We must organize and help one another or else we shall lose out to "them".' Thus emerged a symbiotic relationship between the leaders who aimed to promote personal political ambitions and their followers who craved the rewards that political power entailed; jobs, education and public investment were the prizes.

Tribes and tribalism are in one sense a thoroughly modern creation. The sense of shared identity and interest that defines a tribe was often absent in the precolonial period. Nor were modern antagonists necessarily historical enemies. The bitter rivalry between the Kenyan Luo and Kikuyu is a twentieth-century phenomenon. Indeed, prior to imperial manipulation, neither constituted a distinct ethnic group. There were, instead, acephalous, localized agricultural communities in central Kenya who spoke a mutually intelligible Bantu language and shared cultural beliefs and practices such as female and male circumcision. The Nyeri, Murang'a and Kiambu segments of the Kikuyu were often at war, and sometimes one of these groups would enlist Masai allies. Around Lake Victoria, a similar situation prevailed among the Jaluo-speaking communities. Three conditions which were fulfilled during colonial rule fostered the tribal consciousness of the Kikuyu and Luo peoples: the cultural-linguistic grid of district administration, uneven development and African political competition within the Kenyan colony in the postwar era. Even today the boundaries dividing these groups remain flexible, membership depending upon the arena of competition.

The point is that what is usually labelled ethnicity or tribalism is really the same thing as nationalism. The rivalries engaging the Kikuyu and Luo in Kenya are essentially part of the same parcel as the divisions between the Flemings and the Walloons in Belgium or the French and English in Canada. A sense of cultural uniqueness and a determination to guard mutual interests is the essence of both nationalism and ethnicity. A necessary condition for both is the tangible manifestations of cultural distinctiveness – generally language, and sometimes religion and customs as well. But these traits only become politically salient when aggravated by uneven development, political competition and the self-serving tactics of ambitious politicians. Hence, colonialism was the incubator of Western-style states to be sure, but more significantly, of multinational or polyethnic states.

Ethnic formation was one key aspect of social change during the colonial era; class formation was another. The significance of this latter process lies in the weak articulation of the modern capitalist classes – bourgeoisie and proletariat – and a correspondingly widespread peasantization. This lay the social foundations for a form of patrimonial rule in postcolonial Africa.

All precolonial African societies demonstrated some degree of social differentiation. This stratification was most advanced in the centralized and hierarchical unitary states, for example, the emirates in northern Nigeria and in the less centralized but still pyramidal confederacies such as those amongst the Yoruba. Status distinctions divided these societies into noble, commoner and often slave. In stateless societies such as the Ibo, socio-economic differentiation was considerably less marked.

Regardless of the precolonial social system, imperialism introduced novel bases of social stratification. Western education was one of these. Primary education was principally in the missionaries' hands in British Africa prior to World War II. In French West Africa, the missionary impact was less pronounced owing to a prevalent anticlerical opinion in official circles. Secondary education, crucial in creating a skilled and educated elite, was paid greater heed by the British and French than the Belgians and Portuguese. Renowned institutions of higher learning such as Achimota Secondary School (Gold Coast), Katsina College (Nigeria), Alliance High School (Kenya) and Makerere College (Uganda) were spawned by the British in the 1920s. The French, in the interwar period, opened eight secondary schools in their West and Central African colonies. While the French and British emphasized academic curricula, the Belgians in the Congo and Rwanda-Burundi favoured technical training in post-primary schools. Still, the number of educated Africans was minuscule: in 1960 only three per cent of high-school aged children attended school in subsaharan Africa.

The educated African elite – lawyers, doctors, civil servants, teachers and businessmen – dominated indigenous political associations and anticolonial movements until well into the 1950s. Members of the elite (called *évolué* in French colonies, *immatriculé* in Belgian colonies, *assimilado* in Portuguese Africa and the 'new elite' in British territories) varied widely in number. Whereas in the Gold Coast in the 1920s there were already 60 practising lawyers, Kenya's first African lawyer was not called to the bar until 1956. And even in such a well-endowed colony as the Gold Coast, the intelligentsia constituted only a tiny fraction of the population.

Economic change was another major determinant of social differentiation. Once ensconced in a territory, the imperial power exploited whatever economic potential existed. Each colonial government tried to collect sufficient revenues to cover its expenses and involve at least a few metropolitan firms in lucrative ventures. Northern and Southern Rhodesia (now Zambia and Zimbabwe), South Africa and the Belgian Congo (now Zaire) became major mineral exporters. Other colonies had to be content with more minor mineral exports, usually in addition to peasant or plantation agriculture: the Gold Coast, Sierra Leone, Nigeria, Liberia, Mauritania, Gabon, Guinea and Tanganyika (now Tanzania). Cash crops were the main source of revenue in most territories. European settlers and large plantations produced the bulk of primary exports in settler colonies such as Kenya and South Africa and even in the

Belgian Congo, Northern Rhodesia, Angola and the Ivory Coast. But in most colonies with difficult climatic and health conditions African smallholders carried the burden of agricultural production.

The colonial state played an integral interventionist role, regardless of the particular pattern. It had to lay the ground-work to retrieve mineral reserves and export cash crops. Transport posed a particular problem. Unnavigable rivers, tsetse flies, and devastating tropical storms which flooded roads encouraged railway construction in the early twenti-eth century. The governments used various methods before the Second World War to recruit the necessary cheap labour, including direct coercion (forced labour), indirect compulsion (all male adults were to pay annual taxes), or unfair procedures (labour recruitment through the conniv-ance of chiefs).[4]

In addition, colonial governments built a privileged posi-tion for certain foreign interests. In a few colonies, these were settlers, in others trading companies or concession owners. Kenyan settlers, for example, benefitted substan-tially from the exclusion of Africans from the fertile White Highlands, the ban on African production of coffee, subsi-dies on rail transport, disproportionate allocation of public revenues to European areas and public credit schemes that were denied to Africans. Projects benefitting European interests were often financed by revenues disproportionate-ly squeezed from Africans. A principal means of extracting such revenues was the marketing board, which consistently paid peasants below the world price for their cocoa, coffee, cotton or other crops. In addition, governments allowed European firms to monopolize the most lucrative sector of economic life, the import–export trade, thus blocking a potentially important source of local accumulation.

Economic growth in the postwar period was truly excep-tional.[5] Stoked by high world demand for raw materials, the economies of colonial Africa expanded by four to six per cent per annum between 1945 and 1960. And some areas boasted the highest growth rates in the world: Kenya, the Rhodesias, Gabon and the Belgian Congo saw their GNPs soar between six and eleven per cent per year. Living standards spiralled, but so did popular demands for improved services and opportunities for Africans.

Social stratification was radically altered by these two generations or so of economic change. The European caste formed the apex of colonial societies in terms of wealth and power. Included in this elite were colonial officials, army officers, commercial leaders, white settlers and, occasionally, missionaries. Occupying a step further down the ladder was another alien caste in many colonies – the Syrians and Lebanese in West Africa and the Indians in the East, Central and South Africa. They tended to fill the middle positions in commerce, the civil service and construction and industry. Important as they were in economic life, they constituted only one or, at most, two per cent of territorial populations.

The amorphous African middle class or urban elite was, in the interwar period, tiny and composed mainly of those with some Western education. As the higher administrative ranks in the colonial civil services opened to Africans in the postwar era, this urban elite expanded. Professionals were the dominant element, especially in West Africa where wealthy urban families had sent their sons abroad to university since the early decades. Big businessmen were fewer in number because of the colonial restrictions on African enterprise to favour the white settlers or foreign capital.[6] In effect, African businessmen could accumulate capital only by moving into high risk or less profitable ventures – such as small-scale commerce, cash cropping or transport – that metropolitan capital shunned. These conditions did not favour the emergence of a robust African bourgeoisie.

Ironically, the indigenous bourgeoisie emerged the

strongest precisely where Africans had been most repressed before independence – namely, Southern Rhodesia and Kenya. The settlers exploited the people, but they invested the fruits of that exploitation locally. Colonies with large European populations boasted superior infrastructure, more people involved in markets and relatively substantial local accumulation in capital-intensive estates and manufacturing firms. And because a considerable proportion of the male population was accustomed to wage labour at independence, postcolonial capitalism developed on a firmer base in Kenya and Southern Rhodesia than elsewhere.

A semi-proletarianized labour force thus also evolved. This constituted a drastic departure from traditional African perspectives on the role and division of labour.

Initially, Africans only reluctantly entered the capitalist enclaves as sellers of labour. Traditionally, labour was an obligation one owed as a member of a household and kinship-unit, not a commodity to be sold and purchased on the market. Labour was allocated to specific tasks on the basis of sex and age. Women were responsible for certain domestic and farming duties until they were too infirm to work. Age, not capital, skills or strength, prescribed males' tasks. In pastoral societies, boys of five or six were given charge of a few goats and calves; older boys handled larger herds. The elders were busy with decision-making. In many societies, slaves featured in the prevailing division of labour. They were generally absorbed into the household, the principal unit of agricultural production; eventually, they or their children were accorded the full rights of free men and women.

It was colonialism which radically altered this conception of work. Africans had to adapt to a wage-labour system in which one's productive capacity is sold to the highest bidder. Various methods of physical and indirect coercion were used to generate cheap labour in the colonial period. In the interwar period, most labour migration was on a rural-to-rural basis as work opened up in mines, large public works projects, plantations and prosperous farms. The drift turned toward the booming towns after the war as commerce, social-services bureaucracies and manufacturing expanded. Numerically, though, these migrant workers were always a small group, accounting for only five to ten per cent of the economically active population.

The peasantry was by far the largest group to grow out of the colonial experience. Even today, about three-quarters of Africa's people live on the land. And most are still peasants rather than communal cultivators or commercial farmers. (We summarize these distinctions in Table 5.) Communal cultivators dominated most precolonial societies. Markets in land and labour were nonexistent, though, particularly in West Africa, village market places to exchange the products of household labour were plentiful. The distinction between peasants and communal farmers is a fundamental one. Although still relying principally on family labour, peasants produce not only for the household, but also for a national or international market and to fulfil their obligations to a state elite. In this sense, peasants were largely the product of a commercialization of agriculture begun under colonial auspices. True, pockets of peasants did emerge prior to European domination, for example, in the emirates of northern Nigeria and in Ethiopia and Buganda. Also, some Africans were drawn into the market prior to formal colonial rule in the nineteenth century as they produced such exports for Europe as palm oil, groundnuts and cotton, and later, rubber. But the peasantry didn't expand and stratify into rich and poor segments until the twentieth century.

The colonial state promoted export cash crops to develop local revenues. Some – cocoa, coffee, cotton, groundnuts and palm oil – were suitable for small-scale production, and thus new opportunities opened up to rural Africans. That smallholders would seize these became increasingly likely owing to such changes as the circulation of money, the development of tastes for manufactured products and the imposition of colonial taxes. In these ways, Africans were lured into the world economy without, however, being fully incorporated as commercial farmers – or for that matter, proletarians.[7]

Some peasants, more successful than others, made the full transition to commercial farming. This entailed expanded landholdings and the hiring of labour, that is, a fuller involvement in the capitalist economy. But African commercial farmers were rare at independence.

Social stratification, in short, proceeded apace during the colonial period. But can one validly talk of class formation? If one means simply the formation of large-scale aggregates of people sharing a common role in the process of production and distribution, this is certainly legitimate. Several new classes in this sense have been created by economic and social change as we have seen: chiefly, a middle class (or, more specifically, an intelligentsia and an embryonic petty bourgeoisie), a semi-proletarianized working class, a peasantry and a tiny capitalist farmer class.

But this economistic concept of class, the view that economic forces make classes, will not suffice. We must identify the prime political agency or agencies if we wish to understand the social foundations of African political life. In other words, is political conflict in Africa primarily class conflict, or ethnic or communal conflict? Or are both important sources of cleavage? Classes can, obviously, constitute political agents and engage in conflict only when they gain some subjective reality, that is, when their members feel a sense of common identity, recognize shared interests and organize accordingly.[8] What, then, was the extent of class consciousness and organization in colonial Africa?

Table 5. *Distinctions among rural cultivators*

Traits	Communal cultivator	Peasant	Commercial farmer
1. *land*	communally held	privately owned in practice by landlord or cultivator	privately owned, land an 'asset'
2. *labour*	labour an obligation; division of labour based on kinship, sex and age	labour an obligation; reliance on family labour	'free' labour hired
3. *market*	market places exist but market principle (ie, price formation by impersonal forces of supply and demand) is absent	market principle applies in part	wholly reliant on market
4. *the state*	contingent aspect	exists and extracts surplus	exists to maintain market conditions

Source: Adapted from K. Post, '"Peasantization" and Rural Political Movements in Western Africa', *European Journal of Sociology*, XIII, 2 (1972), 229.

Freedom Now! – the struggle for self-government – was the focus of the most intense political conflict in postwar Africa. What can we learn from this struggle about the social foundations of political life? In fact, both tribe *and* class figured in the political mobilization of African populations, though their relative importance varied with the territory.

On the one hand, ethnic consciousness was masked, but not submerged in the struggle. Sadly, we now understand how misleading it was to romanticize anticolonial movements under the rubric of the 'rise of African nationalism'. A single national consciousness did not unite these ethnically heterogeneous movements. In reality, they were more akin to a coalition of diverse ethnic nationalisms against a common enemy than they were a national movement. Ethnic or regional loyalties were formally recognized by some parties such as the *Parti Démocratique de la Côte d'Ivoire* in their organizational structure: others such as the Kenya African National Union informally channelled these loyalties through ethnic arithmetic in the allocation of leadership positions. In some territories, most strikingly in Nigeria and the Belgian Congo, ethnic tensions translated directly into a proliferation of ethnically based nationalist parties.

These coalitions often unravelled as colonial control lessened with the approach of independence. Where no single tribe threatened to dominate by dint of numbers or economic or educational advantage, Tanganyika, for example, this was less apt to happen. Similarly, the glue held most firmly in colonies whose independence struggle was long and bloody; for through shared tragedy they had built some national solidarity. But ethnic consciousness and its attendant cleavages resurged even in the revolutionary countries of Guinea-Bissau, Zimbabwe, Angola and Mozambique after independence, though in the last three cases with South African connivance.

On the other hand, class elements were not lacking in the anticolonial struggle. We are not suggesting that nationalist parties were simply tools of class interests. After all, these parties directed their appeal to the people in general, and their membership, or at least support, was mainly peasant and working class. The leaders could win extensive popularity only by adopting a militantly populist rhetoric and articulating the grievances of the ordinary people. The strategy was a simple one; identify the colonialists as the stumbling block to the advancement of all classes, strata and regional or ethnic groups.

This approach was a success. But there *was* an element of class struggle. Amongst the educated middle class or emergent petty bourgeoisie there was a clearer recognition of their group interests than amongst the peasants or even workers; they cleverly used the anticolonial parties to realize these special concerns and achieved broader goals as well.

Consider the case of the Gold Coast/Ghana. One influential book has identified the dominant nationalist party, the Convention Peoples' Party (CPP), as an instrument of the petty bourgeoisie.[9] The old urban intelligentsia of professionals, administrators and businessmen formed the first protonationalist associations in the Gold Coast as in most of West Africa in the interwar period. Reformist in spirit, such associations as the National Congress of British West Africa were rather narrowly concerned with the advancement of the African middle class. An amorphous petty bourgeoisie challenged this elitist group and the chiefs after the war. This stratum of clerks, primary-school teachers, health personnel, artisans, mechanics and unemployed school-leavers expanded with the rapid economic growth of this period. One clever politician, Kwame Nkrumah, adroitly mobilized these 'youngmen' in his breakaway CPP to eclipse the more moderate United Gold Coast Convention led by the elite between 1949 and 1951. Roger Genoud writes:

More educated than most chiefs and more frustrated than the intelligentsia, they [the youngmen] formed an aggressively dynamic group.

While the power of the chiefs was limited geographically [...] and the prestige of the intelligentsia leadership was restricted [...] the youngmen found themselves much closer to the mass of the people throughout the country, in the urban zones as well as the rural zones.[10]

They were thus a potent cadre for the CPP.

Was the victory of the CPP in the election of 1951 also a triumph of the petty bourgeoisie over the intelligentsia of professionals and established businessmen? There is some truth in this statement. But this interpretation should not be pushed too far. The CPP was not simply a tool of any class: it articulated the grievances of all sectors and, generally, the will to be free of colonialism. Moreover, this petty bourgeoisie was a class only in the loosest sense. Its membership was defined more by educational achievement than by a common role in the production process.

Furthermore, the major interest shared by this petty bourgeoisie was a desire to *escape* their present status. 'They had no class interest to defend, for, precisely they had nothing, or what they had, they did not want any longer.'[11] Frustration drew the youngmen to the militant CPP. Their modicum of education was insufficient to carve out a suitable position in colonial society. They believed their frustrations would end with the demise of colonialism, when they could rightfully displace or join the old elite. There was, therefore, an element of quasi-class conflict in these struggles; however, given the flux of Ghanaian society at that time, class relationships in no sense are the key to understanding political conflict in general.

This is then how matters stood on the eve of independence. An alien state, a weakly articulated class structure, resurgent ethnic rivalries, high popular expectations – not an auspicious climate for postcolonial progress.

§ 4 §

CLASS, TRIBE AND POLITICS

How do class and tribe affect politics in Africa today? Some writers, mainly Marxists, define class conflicts as the primary contradictions in Africa. They relegate intraclass struggle involving ethnicity or religion to the less important category of 'secondary' contradictions. Other writers, mainly conservatives, see communal conflicts everywhere. They dismiss the significance of class on the grounds that self-conscious classes do not exist. Both of these approaches are unduly reductionist. Neither class nor tribe alone is the key to unravelling African politics. Both must be taken seriously as independent though interacting principles of political mobilization.

What emerged from colonial rule were overwhelmingly peasant, not capitalist, societies. Peasants are notoriously difficult to mobilize on a national class basis. In Africa, they generally do not confront an obvious class enemy in the countryside; social stratification has not yet crystallized sharp rural class divisions. There is a small sector of capitalist production, mainly in the cities. However, the modern capitalist classes, the bourgeoisie and the proletariat, are still embryonic. Class alone fails to explain African political life.

Ethnicity is often of greater political saliency than class. Tribalism is not, as some have assumed, a transitory phenomenon, soon to be displaced by class solidarities.

Ethnic conflicts, sometimes coupled with religious divisions, will continue to undermine a sense of national purpose. Patriotism fails to unite sectional interests in defence of a broad national vision.

Societies with such characteristics are difficult to govern. The stage is set for a strongman to play the central integrating role. He overcomes political schisms and builds his personal rule by distributing material benefits, capitalizing on personal loyalties and coercing recalcitrants. Appeals on a class or patriotic basis are unsuccessful.

Consider first the extent of class formation and class conflict in postcolonial Africa. What are the class dynamics of peasant societies?

Peasantization was the major thrust of colonial economic change. Smallholders in growing numbers were drawn into the money economy as cash crop producers and migratory labourers. But their incorporation into the market was only partial; peasants retained a foot in subsistence farming and the option of withdrawing entirely from the market when agricultural prices plummeted.

At independence, there was a resurgence of peasant agriculture even in the few settler colonies which had developed a substantial commercial farmer sector. Take Kenya, for example. After *uhuru* in 1963, the White Highlands were rapidly Africanized. Under the Million-Acre Schemes, Africans resettled in low- and high-density farming schemes and even purchased land outside these areas on a 'willing seller, willing buyer' basis. The land registers suggest that a good number of commercial farms survived in African hands, but appearances are misleading. Although one or two individuals might hold the land's legal title, in fact it was often subdivided amongst a number of related households, a feature typical of peasant society. As Colin Leys observes: 'The most obvious feature of the whole rural sector is that the peasant farm economy and society has moved far into the former white highlands, engulfing its periphery and penetrating its core.'[1]

Historically, peasant societies have rarely manifested advanced class consciousness on a national basis. In feudal Europe, the aristocracy came closest to evincing a 'national' class consciousness. But even here, the principal criteria of class identity were not economic; this identity stemmed instead from kinship, special legal status, relationship to monarch and so on. For the ordinary rural people, reality lay at the local level. The rest of the world seemed remote and somehow menacing. 'So far as men living in such circumstances are concerned, the man from the next valley may not be merely a foreigner, but an enemy, however similar his situation.'[2] Occasionally, this parochial perspective gave way to a millenarian movement spurring a global consciousness that transcended class. This might take the form of 'countrymen' or '*le menu peuple*'. 'The unit of their organized action is either the parish pump or the universe. There is nothing in between.'[3] Not until the appearance of the modern industrial era, and the rise of the bourgeoisie and the proletariat, was national class consciousness born.

African peasant society discourages the emergence of class consciousness and class conflict in three ways. First, extractions of economic surplus* from peasants do not create the same tensions as in capitalist societies. True, the urban elites benefit from the taxing of a smallholder production and advantageous rural–urban terms of trade; but these extractive mechanisms are indirect, impersonal and inconspicuous. The direct expropriation of a share of the harvest by a landlord is rare. Second, for several reasons, inequality amongst landholders creates few tensions. In Africa, there are few of the glaring differences in land-holdings that distinguish the landed oligarchy from the peasantry in Latin America or Ethiopia before the revolution. Or if there is a landed class, it is numerically small and geographically concentrated, as in the former White Highlands of Kenya. The lines of rural cleavage are thus shadowy. More importantly, kinship still retards the emergence of antagonistic rural classes; rich peasants feel obliged to assist their poor relations and the poor expect this help. And third, class divisions are still fluid. As everyone seems to know of a cousin or friend of a friend who rose above his humble background, even those peasants who are left behind can hope for their children's success. The rapid and widespread upward mobility which the first postcolonial generation enjoyed encouraged a belief in the possibility of upward mobility.

Rural dwellers are not politically quiescent, however. Colonial histories chronicle many instances of rural resistance: of riots sparked by new taxes; of cocoa holdups and associated boycotts of European goods to protest unfair monopolistic pricing policies; of endorsement of nationalist parties and liberation struggles. Peasants have swelled the ranks of anticolonial guerrilla movements in Angola, Cameroon, Guinea-Bissau, Kenya, Mozambique, South Africa and Zimbabwe. In the postindependence era, rural revolts have been few and largely a reflection of ethnic rivalries. The Kwilu rebellion in rural Congo (Zaire) in 1964–5 does not neatly conform to this ethnic pattern, nor does the rebellion in western Nigeria in 1968–9. Both these insurrections, though precipitated by particular government policies, constituted revolts against an urban elite which was popularly construed to be parasitical and corrupt.[4] But the resistance soon petered out, lacking as it did a revolutionary programme.

Rural protests exist and they unite all but the wealthiest rural dwellers into a single movement. These are rebellions against some outside force, an urban elite or colonial power – not cases of class conflict. Class consciousness and struggle are more children of the city, the breeding place of capitalism, of bourgeoisie and proletariat. How does each of these evolve within the bosom of peasant society?

For the indigenous bourgeoisie, independence meant more freedom for its expansion. Colonialism constrained African accumulation in a number of ways, but no longer would the state favour foreign over local interests. African entrepreneurs were at last to have their day, except where power passed to the socialists.

The state has constituted the principal instrument of personal advancement. The bureaucracy has not only formulated economic policy – it has been the main beneficiary of this as well. This story is now a familiar one. The upper echelons of the civil service, along with politicians and the business partners of these two groups, avidly exploited the new economic opportunities. They held a number of advantages including relatively high salaries, easy access to public and private credit and the willingness of government agencies to facilitate their economic success. And the unscrupulous could tap unethical or illicit financial sources, as growing public participation in economic life extended the bureaucrats' field of manoeuvre. Regulatory agencies, marketing boards and public corporations proliferated. Opportunities for corruption were legion as officials were called upon to exercise more authority – grant permits and licences, tender contracts, regulate commercial transactions, direct corporations and invest public revenues.

These advantages allowed political insiders to become property owners or to augment the assets they formerly controlled. Urban real estate is ever a popular investment. As city size exploded, enormous profits could be made from land speculation, office construction and the rental of houses improperly acquired in low-income site-and-service schemes or constructed in swank suburbs. Investors were also attracted to farms and estates managed by relatives or expatriate experts. This was especially true in the former colonies where settlers had developed large commercial farms. Farms were also a lucrative investment in countries such as the Ivory Coast and Nigeria with a high demand for foodstuffs and/or crops for export. By providing cheap credit and expert extension services, the state assisted local land accumulation.

Another particularly rewarding venture was indigenous involvement in commerce and manufacturing, often in joint ventures with transnational corporations or through the purchase of their shares. Local entrepreneurs were encouraged by the public sector through indigenization laws restricting certain economic activities to citizens, pressure on transnationals to sell shares in local subsidiaries or commit themselves to joint ventures, credit facilities and advisory and training services for businessmen.[5]

These facts are not the subject of dispute. But what conclusions can be drawn? Did the state facilitate local accumulation in response to the interests of a dominant or ruling class? Or was the state the instrument of a political elite attempting to translate its political power into economic prosperity? In other words, is the indigenous bourgeoisie a dominant class in Marxian terms or merely an embryonic class at most, dependent upon political power for its survival and expansion? A definitive answer is out of the question; situations vary and the criteria for judging class crystallization are imprecise. Nonetheless, the latter interpretation seems more persuasive.

Some respected writers have, however, argued the contrary position with respect to certain key countries. Leys observes:

When circumstances permit an indigenous capitalist class to establish itself effectively in power, as in the Ivory Coast and Kenya, the conditions for capitalist development at the hands of both foreign and domestic capital are enormously enhanced.[6]

Here then, is the clear image of the state as 'importantly conditioned by a domestic class with substantial capital of its own at stake'.[7]

Does this dominant capitalist class hold power in Kenya, for example? Yes, a prominent school informs us. At independence, the indigenous bourgeoisie acceded to power and rapidly accumulated capital aided by a favourable combination of circumstances. For one, the indigenous, largely Kikuyu, accumulators from the colonial period survived. This group had exploited opportunities in the interstices of the settler-controlled economy, and formed the kernel of Kenya's dominant class. A second beneficial factor was the settlers' success at undermining precapitalist forms of production, forming a large labour market, building an advanced economic infrastructure and accumulating capital in farms and factories. On this groundwork, an indigenous bourgeoisie built, helped by the postcolonial state it controlled. Its members assumed positions formerly held by Europeans and established control over Kenya's petty bourgeoisie, peasantry and labour. Bourgeois class consciousness was apparent not only in this use of the state, but in the parallel development of bourgeois culture.[8]

This is a plausible position. But other evidence casts doubt on this explanation of the state's role by reference to the independent class power of a national bourgeoisie. First, how does the expansion of peasant agriculture at the expense of commercial farms jibe with the notion of a rising bourgeoisie? Surely this is the reverse of what one would reasonably expect in these circumstances.

Secondly, there is the question of hegemony. To establish itself effectively in power, a bourgeoisie must control a state that governs through the consent of the lower classes. This in turn means that the values of the rising class must suffuse society to the point that they are held universally. Hegemony in this sense contrasts with supremacy based on domination, that is, the state's reliance upon forced obedience.[9] But in Kenya, no social class has become hegemonic. Wealthy businessmen are the envy of many peasants, workers and unemployed, who dream of joining their ranks. This does not mean, however, that they have absorbed the instrumental and individualistic ethic of capitalism. Individual competition, personal accumulation, thrift, rational calculation of means and ends, efficiency, innovation – these Calvinist values have not penetrated deeply into a peasant society rooted in an 'economy of affection'.[10] Its values are traditional ones such as solidarity with kin, the minimization of risks and household autonomy.

Have bourgeois values suffused even the Kenyan bourgeoisie? The answer, according to a group of radical Kenyan critics, is no. Their 'ruling class' is dismissed in stinging and contemptuous terms:

Indifferent to the bourgeois values that made European society so dynamic in the nineteenth century – to a respect for thrift, hard work and punctuality – our leaders operate with a pre-capitalist mentality. They embrace the type of conspicuous consumption which is the hallmark of the feudal ruling caste, where the patron has to impress his dependent clients with the hollow pomp and lavish signs of wealth and influence. They respect the big belly squeezed under the steering wheel of the Mercedes far more than they respect talent, quality and productivity. Perpetual parasites, they are simply not good enough to be truly bourgeois.[11]

What makes the Kenyan bourgeoisie's class power seem comparatively formidable is two factors. The first is the cohesiveness and cultural distinctiveness of this group. But this owes much to the Kikuyu domination of African big business. Kikuyu preponderance can be attributed to several factors: their headstart, in education and jobs, during colonial rule; their numbers (twenty per cent of the population); their geographical location in the heartland of the country; and, under Kenyatta's leadership, their domination of the ruling Kenya African National Union (KANU).

Secondly, the Kikuyu elite benefitted from the considerable assets built up in colonial Kenya by settlers, Asian
capitalists and transnationals. This political elite could, and
did, use the state to displace or ally itself with European or
Asian capital. Its members accumulated a substantial
economic stake during the sixties and seventies.

But the Kenyan bourgeoisie is not a dominant or ruling
class in the Western European mould. The Kikuyu elite's
political power in the anticolonial movement allowed it to
build its economic power, not vice versa. This economic
power is limited by the fact that the bourgeoisie is not a
national class. Under the presidency of Daniel arap Moi, a
Kalenjin, it became disadvantageous to be a Kikuyu. By
1983, the Kikuyu were a minor force within Moi's system of
personal rule. The President surrounded himself with the
leaders of smaller tribes who, in turn, used the state apparatus to displace the Kikuyu bourgeoisie. Based as it was on
patronage and force, Kikuyu dominance proved vulnerable
to the turns of political fortune.

One must also be sceptical about a strong national
bourgeoisie in that other exemplar of African capitalism,
the Ivory Coast. By 1980, for instance, private Ivorian
interests owned only 11 per cent of manufacturing capital,
while foreign firms owned 36 per cent and the state 53 per
cent. Ivorian private capital was concentrated in a mere
handful of agro-industries.[12] These figures starkly reveal the
economic weakness of the Ivorian capitalist class.

Perhaps, though, this class bases itself on agriculture. In
the sixties and seventies, many speculated that a planto-
cracy actually ran the show. This was the social force that
apparently provided the leadership under Félix Houphouët-
Boigny of the *Parti Démocratique de la Côte d'Ivoire*.
According to recent research, a different picture emerges; *la
bourgeoisie de planteurs*, that is, the commercial farmers, is
tiny, heterogeneous and no longer composed of the old
guard of colonial days. Instead, the usual pattern of a

political elite constituted of politicians and bureaucrats who use their positions to move into capitalist farming obtains.[13] The state, again, shapes economic opportunities in a fluid social situation. Thus, the story is the same in the Ivory Coast; a national bourgeoisie is only embryonic and dependent on state power.

What conclusions can we draw? One is left with the proposition that 'class relations, at bottom, are determined by relations of power, not production'.[14] But let us be clear on what this position entails – it undercuts the whole basis of Marxist class analysis. Fundamental to this is the notion that the economic power of a class conditions the exercise of political power, though the state retains a vague political autonomy. What remains of this concept when the formula is reversed? In effect, we are designating as the dominant or ruling class a political elite which aspires to become a bourgeoisie. But this aspiration itself connotes little more than an opportunistic exploitation of 'insider' privileges in many cases (e.g., Nigeria, Ghana, Uganda, Zaire), not the development of the classic risk-taking entrepreneurial behaviour. Moreover, this embryonic 'bourgeoisie' is not only recent in origin but thoroughly dependent on the state for protection from foreign capital, control of the labour force, loan capital and so on. A concept such as dominant class, which assumes the primacy of economic power, can be highly misleading in these circumstances.

Nonetheless, the weakness of other classes enhances the political weight of the emergent bourgeoisie/political elite. The peasantry, while large in numbers, lacks political influence as a class due to the absence of autonomous organization and regional/ethnic divisions. More potent is foreign capital. Yet its power is mainly negative – a capacity to evade policies contrary to its interests (see Chapter 6). The only competing indigenous class organized on a national basis is the working class. However, its political influence too is vitiated by various factors. Let us consider these now.

The African working class is relatively small. The proportion of economically active people in wage employment ranges from at least a quarter in Zambia to less than five per cent in Mali or Niger. As much as half of urban labour forces are modern-sector workers.[15]

Though small, the urban wage-earning force has recently stabilized. During the colonial period, most workers fluctuated between town and country. But since the fifties, those with jobs have tried to hold on to them. A long-term need for cash, growing land shortages, massive unemployment and underemployment all encouraged labour stability. In the modern sector, the turnover rate in 1980 was comparable to industrial countries.

But these urban workers are only partially proletarianized. That is, they are not wholly dependent on their jobs for their survival. Many retain rights to land, even if they work in the city until retirement age. A half or more of workers have rights to land in their rural homelands, according to various surveys.

This continuing access encourages workers to retain their rural bonds:

Throughout Subsaharan Africa urban dwellers regularly visit their rural homes where they bring gifts, find wives, maintain land rights, build houses, intend to retire eventually, want to be buried; they receive gifts, offer hospitality to visitors from home, and help new arrivals in town.[16]

A typical worker remits as much as one-fifth of his take-home pay to rural kin, and supports village improvement societies and urban ethnic associations. In these ways, wage-earners try to safeguard their land rights and procure an honoured position for themselves in their home areas. As such, rural links are a rational response to an insecure urban life.

What are the implications of this semi-proletarianization for workers' consciousness? First and even second generation workers are men and women of two worlds. They can afford to ignore neither village politics nor urban problems; traditional ties must consume their emotional energies as much as do unemployment, wages and the cost of living. Since the latter are the issues which engage trade unions, even semi-proletarianized African workers have an interest in trade unionism and worker solidarity. But does such solidarity ever assume a radical political direction? In practice, African unions concentrate overwhelmingly on the workers' immediate economic interests. That is partly because African governments are notoriously hostile to dissident labour organizations and quite repressive. Beyond that, radical workers' consciousness and action are discouraged by the pull of communal identities within national political arenas.

Workers on their own have, however, spearheaded populist outbursts. But populism is not specifically a working-class consciousness. Rather, it is a mentality of the underclasses as a whole. Its prime feature is a dichotomous 'we–them' world view: 'they' – an allegedly corrupt and supercilious elite – are said to be personally responsible for an unjust and oppressive social order; all virtue resides in 'us' – the common folk. Populism does not reject the prevailing value system. It merely demands that the powerful respect this in practice. It attempts to change the people who govern, not the system itself.

The general or wildcat strike which supplements its economic demands with a political critique is, in Africa, the quintessence of workers' populist protest. African labour history records many instances, a few as early as the turn of the century, in which the striking workers crystallized the inchoate socio-political grievances of the common people.[17] When such strikes garnered widespread popular participation and support, they constituted ephemeral protest movements against colonial or postcolonial ruling circles.

The political impact of strikes in Africa is disproportionate to the relatively small number of workers involved. This is because the legitimacy of regimes is often tenuous, and the workers are concentrated within the urban seats of power where disaffected urban poor are likely to swell their ranks during disturbances.

Strikes have been a major dimension of the urban protest that threatened or toppled governments in many countries: in Senegal in 1968, Ghana in 1950, 1961 and 1971, Nigeria in 1945, 1964 and 1981, the Congo-Brazzaville in 1963 and 1968, the Sudan in 1958, 1964 and 1985, Madagascar in 1972 and Ethiopia in 1974. The political impact of these strikes depended upon their links with other protests and demonstrations, especially those organized by university and secondary school students. In some cases such as Congo-Brazzaville, the Sudan, Madagascar and Ethiopia general strikes formed part of the background to an overthrow of government, but power passed to the army, not the workers.

Workers, particularly dockers, railwaymen, miners and factory hands, have sometimes been the leading edge of popular resentment. This is not surprising, as workers have a peculiar facility for organized action. In the context of a struggle against a common employer, dockers, miners, railwaymen and factory workers develop a sense of solidarity. Their interaction on the job, and often off the job too, reinforces a common identity and outlook. Their concentration in one or a few work-places facilitates communication and organization. The workers' trade union experience at the grass roots solidifies cohesion and organizational skills. For the purposes of leading protests, these workers are consequently more advantageously placed than the petty bourgeois, subproletarian and unemployed elements. For the latter strata are actually in competition in the marketplace and divided by the absence of a cooperative labour process.

Populism, however, is a limited ideology. It fosters only protests against a corrupt, self-interested political elite, not concerted political action to control or reshape institutions. And the spasmodic and localized nature of populist protest undercuts its political import. Normally, regimes can easily quell disorganized unrest; repression, concessions and verbal sympathy for populist rhetoric usually do the trick. And even when such rebellions do occasionally unseat governments, power falls to the only group with the organization to exercise it – the military.

Populism is, therefore, at most a quasi-class struggle. Workers' propensity for populist protest is a function of their only partial proletarianization. At this early phase of industrialization, they retain strong kinship and friendship links with the peasants and urban poor. Indeed, if unemployment befalls them, they rejoin these comrades. Workers are still, above all, men and women of the people.

Because both modern capitalist classes are typically embryonic in these peasant societies, class takes us only so far in coming to terms with African politics. Of course, the rate at which the bourgeoisie and proletariat form varies from country to country. The process is much more evolved in Nigeria than Niger, for example. Generally, though, another principle of political organization – ethnicity or, more broadly, communalism – is more politically salient than class.

Ethnic consciousness, we must affirm, is neither irrational nor ephemeral.[18] From the perspective of the ordinary people, ethnicity appears no less sensible a basis for political mobilization than class. Ethnic mobilization is, after all, just a means to an end, a way of forging a coalition to pursue scarce material benefits. Governments are in the business of allocating resources. Public officials must decide where to locate clinics, schools, wells, roads, market places and so on. And these same people distribute plum jobs, government contracts, publicly funded loans and licences. Groups manoeuvre to influence these crucial decisions. And ethnicity in many countries provides a ready-made vehicle through which to work.

Ethnicity is, moreover, a surprisingly flexible basis for political solidarity. Boundaries of a tribe or ethnic group are not clearly demarcated once and for all. Ethnic self-definition varies depending upon the arena of competition. Within the context of the Central Province of Kenya, the divisions among the Kiambu, Murang'a and Nyeri Kikuyu are salient. But in the national arena of Nairobi and the central government, Kikuyu often perceive themselves as a distinct group in competition with the Luo or other tribes.

Ethnicity is also not transitory. As we emphasized in Chapter 3, it is a modern, not an atavistic, phenomenon or a product merely of cultural diversity or traditional hostilities. Ethnic consciousness has grown since the turn of the century along with uneven development and individual and group competition in new territorial arenas. There is no sign that it is on the wane.

Indeed, in most African countries today the incidence of ethnically based conflict is high. In a few instances, ethnic lines of cleavage have coincided with class lines and promoted a revolutionary situation. In Zanzibar, for example, the poor African majority was controlled by a traditional, almost exclusively Arab, oligarchy before and during the colonial period. In 1964, this Arab elite was overthrown and the revolutionaries installed an initially radical African regime.

And this is not a unique situation. Both Burundi and Rwanda, former Belgian territories, have experienced violent attempts by the Hutu majorities (85 per cent of the population) to repudiate their serf-like subordination to the Tutsi aristocracies. At the cost of as many as 200,000 lives, the Tutsi repulsed an uprising in Burundi in 1972. This episode ignited renewed interethnic battle in neighbouring Rwanda, where the Tutsi were ousted by the Hutu in 1961 in another bloody insurrection. Although tension is considerable, the Tutsi still control Burundi.

In other countries, ethnic rivalries have exploded into civil wars in which class factors were relatively unimportant. Zaire has survived sectional struggles which date back to independence. Katanga fought to free itself from Kinshasa's control during two periods in the sixties. And the war was rekindled in 1977 and again in 1978 with two invasions of Katanga (Shaba) by Katangan exiles from Angola. Only French and Belgian military intervention rescued the client regime in Kinshasa.

A similar situation exists in the Sudan. In a bloody civil war of nine years, Anyanya guerrillas fought for secession of the Black South from the Arabized North. The war terminated with an agreement granting such concessions as regional self-government for the South. But when Khartoum unilaterally revoked this agreement in 1983, the warfare began again twenty years after the initial outburst under a reconstituted 'Anyanya II'.

Ethiopia has been plagued with civil wars since 1962. When the Eritreans were fully incorporated into the Ethiopian Empire, contrary to agreement, they fought for the right to secede. That war continues today; perhaps 15,000 Eritrean guerrillas bear arms. The Somalis of the Ogaden region opened up a second front in 1974 because they wanted to be annexed to Somalia. Foreign powers have involved themselves, too; with Soviet and Cuban assistance in 1978, Ethiopia reestablished control of the Ogaden. But sporadic fighting continues there, as well as in Tigrean areas.

Chad was another battleground for ethnic nationalism. Civil war began in 1965, pitting the Arabic North against

he Black South. The culmination in 1980 was a victory
for the Northern forces followed by a persistent armed
struggle amongst Northern guerrilla leaders for pre-
eminence.

Nigeria, too, has been embroiled in a bloody civil war. An
Ibo army battled the federal forces from 1967–70 to win the
right to secede and found the Republic of Biafra. Tens of
thousands of people died before Biafra collapsed from a
shortage of supplies and manpower and utter exhaustion in
December 1969.

Uganda's plight is certainly one of the most ugly. At first,
sporadic fighting involved mainly the Baganda of the South
against the North. Later, Northern tribes struggled against
each other. Now the Southern peoples again are in a struggle against a dominant North. The hostilities which have
convulsed the country since 1965 have devastated its people.

Less dramatic but more common is the involvement of
ethnic solidarities in the day to day manoeuvrings of political intrigue. Such activity is normally contained within the
bounds of non-violent competition. But when tensions
mount, there are sporadic breakdowns; consider the periodic communal rioting in Nigeria's northern cities directed
against non-Muslim 'strangers'.

In a minority of countries, ethnic cleavages are of less
significance. Where no single ethnic group is powerful
enough to control national political institutions and arenas,
this is more likely to be the case. Blessed, indeed, is a country
such as Tanzania with a large number of equally powerful
tribes. Although there are ethnic suspicions and loyalties,
one is less likely to observe ethnic solidarity stimulated by
fear of another tribe's outright domination.

Neither is ethnicity a major source of division in the Ivory
Coast. A large foreign population serves as a scapegoat for
economic and social problems. African aliens, migrants
from such poor countries as Burkina Fasso and Mali, consti-

tute a quarter of the labour force. The most exploited element in the so-called Ivorian miracle, they fill the un-skilled jobs Ivorians reject. In times of tension and disaffection, these foreigners have provided a convenient target for popular hostility. The schism between the Ivorian and foreign elements has eclipsed the divisions among several Ivorian tribes that might otherwise have surfaced.

But more common is the situation in which the masses perceive the state as representing the interests of one dominant tribe or ethnic coalition. People will then see the aim of politics as augmenting the proportion of the political elite drawn from their own tribe and securing a fair share of state benefits for themselves, their region and their communal group.

Governing in these circumstances is tricky. Presidents and lesser politicians will publicly condemn tribalism, resort to 'ethnic arithmetic' in assigning certain governmental positions, propagate patriotism through schools and institute one-party states allegedly in order 'to suppress divisive tendencies'. Privately, though, the leaders may not engage in positive, nation-building tactics. They may surreptitiously try to augment their personal power by the ancient stratagems of divide-and-rule and the consolidation of an ethnic base or ethnic coalition.

Divide-and-rule entails the manipulation of interethnic hostilities in order to neutralize those who might otherwise challenge central authority. A favourite tactic is to decry vehemently the apparent hegemonic or secessionist ambitions of a particular outgroup. In Ghana, for instance, Akan dominated governments have frequently attacked 'Ewe tribalism'. Apparently this stratagem has successfully mobilized interethnic unity against an alleged threat of domination or secession from this minority group (16 percent of the population) without provoking a violent Ewe reaction.[19]

Leaders in Kenya, too, have employed this tactic. Kenyatta obliquely identified the Luo and their champion, Oginga Odinga, as the central threat to national unity in 1966 through 1978. By 1983, the tide had turned; President Daniel arap Moi alluded to the subversive activities of the Kikuyu and Luo as a ploy to consolidate the support of the smaller tribes.

The flip side of divide-and-rule is usually the leader's unacknowledged efforts to erect his base upon the solidarity of a strategically placed tribe or tribal coalition. This has been the case in Uganda since before independence in 1962, regardless of periodic public announcements condemning tribalism. Before Idi Amin's brutal reign of terror (1972–9), Milton Obote's Uganda People's Congress (UPC) was the mouthpiece of the Nilotic tribes, but had little support from the numerous, wealthier and educationally sophisticated Baganda of the South. The earlier pattern reestablished itself in the post-Amin elections held in 1980. The UPC won the election, but was humiliated in Buganda. Since then Obote has repeated another pattern; placing his own Langi tribesmen in the top echelons of the police, army and government, he has tried to consolidate his control. Clearly, this short-run tactic will provoke a backlash by other tribes, undermining further the leader's sense of security.

But ethnicity rarely is so central to political struggle that it eclipses the class factor. The interaction between class and ethnicity is varied and complex. For example, consider this relationship as it appears amongst the urban poor of Northern Nigeria. For the urban *talakawa* of Kano, Islam is the cement of a cultural solidarity among ethnically heterogeneous workers, small artisans and traders. Anyone who practices Islam, speaks Hausa and lives according to the Hausa lifestyle, is accepted as a Hausa. Islam thus facilitates cooperation among poor *talakawa*, as it builds community and a sense of communication amidst ethnic pluralism.

Furthermore, Islam furnishes a familiar language of class conflict: trade unions in Kano have effectively used egalitarian themes from the Koran to justify their industrial actions and demands.[20]

On these foundations – limited class formation in peasant societies, resurgent ethnicity, fragile legitimacy – emerges a political system of personal rule.

§ 5 §

ANATOMY OF PERSONAL RULE

Just how do rulers govern in these circumstances? We have already considered some common strategies to use or neutralize ethnicity and build the economic power of the politically powerful. But governing is a more complex process than this: rulers must motivate bureaucrats to implement laws and policies and citizens to act in accordance with authoritative decisions. How can a governing elite obtain this double compliance in weakly integrated, poverty-stricken peasant societies?

A strong state is one that can count on willing compliance. All rulers desire legitimacy – the conviction among bureaucrats and citizens that they are under an obligation to obey those occupying certain authority-positions. Relatively few governments, however, achieve a firm moral basis for their rule. If legitimacy is fragile, willing compliance must derive from pragmatic considerations. People consent because they believe that a particular government or policy advances their interests. This explains why a ruler surreptitiously favours a strategic region or tribe; he hopes to gain generalized support amongst that group. Beyond that, he buys instrumental allegiance from influential individuals and groups through patronage. Yet, the greater a regime's dependence upon mercenary support, the greater is its vulnerability to disaffection in the event of an economic downturn.

The other basis for rule is, of course, coerced compliance. All governments, to be sure, depend from time to time on some form of coercion; the application of this may fall to the courts, the army, the police or the prisons. But some governments command so little legitimacy and are so ineffectual at handing out the spoils that they depend heavily on force. This unstable and ineffective mode of governing is seen in many African countries.

With independence and the usual decomposition of the anticolonial front, African states suffered a crisis of legitimacy. Politicians, bureaucrats and people in general grew preoccupied with private and sectional advantage. To what principle could leaders now appeal for solidarity and sacrifice? Ideologies that elsewhere facilitate consent, liberalism and socialism, have no roots to sustain them in Africa. And the traditional legitimacy of precolonial politics was largely irrelevant in the culturally heterogeneous modern state. The result was the emergence of personal rule based chiefly upon personal loyalty, patron–client linkages and coercion.

If an African bourgeoisie had emerged and achieved hegemony, then liberal democracy might have provided a moral basis for governance. A strong bourgeoisie might have championed individual liberty and constitutionalism. And a Westminster-style constitution might then have actually mirrored the values of society, or at least a significant portion of it. But this was not to be. Instead, colonial rulers, in partnership with leading Africans, spawned constitutions that had no more basis in local political cultures than the parchment on which they were inscribed. The limitation of governmental powers, the protection of civil liberties, the principles of representative and responsible government – all these found their place. But in country after country following independence, regimes systematically evaded or abolished these safeguards.

Could the story have been different? Certain liberal-democratic values may have existed in traditional societies, but in a much altered guise and more intimate political environment. These new societies' major political traditions were, in fact, derived from the colonial era – a truly autocratic epoch. Colonial government took the form of an authoritarian administrative apparatus, with a powerful governor at the helm. True, decolonization entailed the cautious devolution of power and responsibility to increasingly representative assemblies. But this whole process was brief, rarely lasting longer than ten to 15 years and often less. Social values could not make the radical adjustment to constitutionalism in this short time, especially since that historical proponent of liberal democracy – the bourgeoisie – was so weak. Regimes thus met with little popular resistance in dismantling democratic institutions.

Whatever the specific route, authoritarianism was generally the outcome. Over half of the regimes in 1984 were, as Table 6 shows, military or quasi-military. In practice, it is difficult to distinguish between these forms as army-supported governments often deck themselves out in civilian garb. Military-dominated regimes range from the relatively benign such as Togo and Guinea-Bissau to the relatively brutal in Uganda, Ethiopia and Zaire.

Another third or more of the countries had one-party states or hereditary monarchies. They are not equally autocratic; Tanzania, for instance, is led by a president sincerely committed to his peoples' welfare and by a party which permits some measure of popular choice in the selection of party officials and parliamentarians. Real but limited intraparty competition also occurs in the Ivory Coast, Kenya, Mozambique and Zambia. Other regimes allow no meaningful popular involvement in the political world. These include both governments of the left and right, for example, Sekou Touré's Guinea and Hastings Banda's Malawi respectively.

Competitive party politics are allowed in only five, less

than one-eighth, of these countries. And even in these cases, the tolerance of the governing elite is either tenuous or untested. It is not cynical to wonder if Senegal's ruling Socialist Party would actually hand over the reigns of government if it was constitutionally defeated by a coalition of opposition parties. Since it won 111 of the 120 assembly seats in the February 1983 elections, its tolerance of opposition is untested. And will Zimbabwe's multiparty system survive the next election given Prime Minister Mugabe's declared support for a one-party state?

African hopes for a democratic future were dealt a cruel blow with the successful *coup d'état* against Prime Minister Shehu Shagari's Nigerian government in late 1983. Widespread allegations of electoral rigging by government agents in the August 1983 elections, rampant inflation and revelations of massive political corruption brought the ruling National Party of Nigeria into disrepute and precipitated the army's action. In practice, democratic norms were widely abused.

In sum, the regimes which command willing compliance on the grounds that they respect constitutional procedures are few. Insecurity motivates the incumbents to eliminate the opposition. But on the eve of victory the new elite finds itself naked, without a moral basis for rule. Some regimes still try to claim the legitimacy that stems from adherence to legal norms and a few single-party states have established so-called one-party democracies to buttress their claim. Intra-party elections do offer limited participation. But the strongman is always tempted to intervene surreptitiously to eliminate real or imagined opponents, thus vitiating his democratic pretensions.

This happened in Kenya, for instance. In the September 1983 elections, certain very popular politicians who were perceived as President Moi's opponents, lost their long-held constituencies to unknown opponents. Kenyans widely as-

Table 6. *Type of government, January 1984*

Military	Quasi-Military	1 Party State or Hereditary Monarch	Competitive Party system
Burundi	Benin	Angola	Botswana
Central African Republic	Guinea-Bissau	Cameroon	Gambia
Chad	Mali	Comoros	Mauritius
Congo (Brazzaville)	Somalia	Djibouti	Senegal
Equatorial Guinea	Togo	Gabon	Zimbabwe
Ethiopia	Uganda	Guinea	
Ghana	Zaire	Ivory Coast	
Liberia		Kenya	
Madagascar		Lesotho	
Mauritania		Malawi	
Niger		Mozambique	
Nigeria		Sierra Leone	
Rwanda		Swaziland	
Sudan		Tanzania	
Upper Volta		Zambia	

Source: Author's files

sume that the ballot boxes were tampered with. Whether or not this occurred, the legal basis of Moi's rule had been further eroded.

Revolutionary legitimacy is another moral basis for rule. Citizens and bureaucrats will comply with a regime's directives if they identify with the charismatic mission of the ruler(s). The mission of the left is the construction of socialism. But only a handful of governments have genuinely committed themselves to a radical socialist project – Angola, Ethiopia, Mozambique, Somalia and Tanzania (see

Chapter 1). Moreover, with Ethiopia the only exception, these regimes have pragmatically adjusted in a capitalist direction. This is the result of a complex blend of factors: economic failure, niggardly Soviet aid (except for Ethiopia), pressure from the IMF and World Bank and regional conflicts pitting socialist regimes against each other. Despite economic failure and rampant famine, however, observers report sizeable pockets of popular support for the revolution in Angola, Ethiopia, Mozambique and perhaps Tanzania. Socialism, even with the pressure of harsh economic conditions and without the benefit of a clearly defined class enemy, still holds the loyalty of many.

Tradition is another potential source of legitimacy. Rulers can anticipate willing compliance if they govern in accordance with immemorial prescriptive norms, usually sanctioned by religion. In Chapter 3, we briefly reviewed three distinct forms of traditional political structure: the unitary states of the emirs, the Yoruba confederacies and the acephalous or stateless societies of the Ibo. The first two were variants of what the German sociologist, Max Weber, called patrimonialism.[1] For him, patrimonialism emerged in societies akin to those of the Ibo with the formation of an administrative staff and military force under the personal control of a chief. Patrimonial regimes could take one of two forms: either centralized as with the emirates or decentralized as among the Oyo Yoruba. The latter arose when subordinate leaders established a hereditary claim on certain administrative offices, as in feudal societies where the monarch had to recognize the regional power of the nobles. Those who appropriated offices would support themselves with taxes or booty.

In Africa, traditionalist patrimonial regimes persisted only in those few polities that survived intact the colonial era: Ethiopia – before the overthrow of Emperor Haile Selassie I in 1974, Burundi – before the 1966 *coup d'état*,

Lesotho and Swaziland. The bizarre attempt of former Sergeant Jean Bedel Bokassa to establish a patrimonial kingdom in his renamed Central African Empire is worth mention. He, of course, was to be the self-appointed emperor. This farce was ended several years later in 1979 with a successful *coup* aided by the French military. Elsewhere traditional patrimonialism has not yet emerged, probably because the traditional norms that could sanction it are irrelevant to the large-scale and culturally plural postcolonial state.

Sultanism, as Weber calls it, or personal rule[2] is more relevant to the circumstances of contemporary Africa. This is a form of patrimonialism that arises when rulers have no constitutional, charismatic-revolutionary or traditional legitimacy. A chief or strongman emerges and rules on the basis of material incentives and personal control of his administration and armed force. Fear and personal loyalties are the mainstays of a personalistic government untrammelled by traditional or modern constitutional limitations. Strongmen generally concoct a patina of traditional respectability by introducing familiar political symbols and practices, but the efficacy of this stratagem is debatable.

Personal rule prevails in most African countries today. The major exception is the militantly socialist regimes, such as those in Angola, Mozambique, Guinea-Bissau, Ethiopia and Tanzania, whose revolutionary experiences have forged institutions and commitments that transcend mercenary considerations. Sultanism flourishes elsewhere under a number of guises: civilian, quasi-military or military forms of government, one-party or competitive-party systems or even under the socialist veneer of Guinea, Benin and the Republic of the Congo. A universal element is the strongman, whose composite portrait looks something like this.

The strongman, usually the president, occupies the centre of political life. Front and centre stage, he is the centrifugal force around which all else revolves. Not only the ceremonial head of state, the president is also the chief political, military and cultural figure: head of government, commander-in-chief of the armed forces, head of the governing party (if there is one) and even chancellor of the local university. His aim is typically to identify his person with the 'nation'. His physical self is omnipresent: as in Orwell's *1984*, Big Brother's picture is plastered on public walls, billboards and even private homes. His portrait also adorns stamps, coins, paper money and even the T-shirts and buttons often distributed to the party 'faithful'. Schools, hospitals and stadiums are named after him. The mass media herald his every word and action, no matter how insignificant.

The cult of personality may even extend to an identification of a country's recent history with the wise/heroic/magnanimous deeds and decisions of the leader. For example, officially inspired and distributed comic-book biographies have appeared for Qaddafy (Libya), Mobutu (Zaire), Ahidjo (Cameroon), Bongo (Gabon), Eyadema (Togo), Senghor (Senegal), and Houphouët-Boigny (Ivory Coast). These biographies all treat the leader as hero, vanquishing the colonialists and disreputable domestic foes, benignly building the nation and acting as world statesman. They are generally disseminated through the elementary schools and the ruling party.

The strongman needs – and demands – veneration and obedience. He surrounds himself with followers who constantly reaffirm their faith in his exceptional wisdom and generosity. All or the bulk of strategic positions in the political, bureaucratic, police and military hierarchies are filled with personally loyal individuals. These include relatives, especially close ones such as brothers and cousins, friends and classmates, kinsmen and tribesmen. For these and for other followers, the expectation of sharing in the spoils of office reinforces the personal link to the chief. Kenyan dissidents aptly capture the essence of personal rule in this mocking description of President's Moi's regime:

All power emanates from the centre of the system, from our imperial President. Political success and personal enrichment depend on the positions held by the different planets as they circulate around the sun-king. Since the President, through his control of the state apparatus, bestows access to our country's increasingly scarce resources, the closer the politician-planet to the centre, the more power he can trap and reflect on down to his own satellites and flunkeys. As our politicians orbit endlessly around the President, they compete with each other to sing his praises loudly and attract his favour. Obsequious loyalty brings its own reward...[3]

President Mobutu Sese-Seko of Zaire is an extreme version of a sun-king. In the orbits closest to him circle the dozen or so members of the presidential clique. These are his trusted kinsmen, the men who occupy the most sensitive and lucrative government positions. The presidential brotherhood is somewhat further from the sun. Theirs are the top political and administrative posts and their relationship with the President is symbiotic. He demands their absolute personal allegiance and, in return, grants them access to power and illegal opportunities to accumulate wealth. His displeasure guarantees personal ruin and even imprisonment. The most distant satellites are the thousands of middle-level officials, army officers and university personnel. While their opportunities for aggrandizement are more limited, they can still become well off. And they can aspire to join the presidential brotherhood. Meanwhile, the mass of the population is excluded from the spoils and subject to repression.[4]

Mobutu, like all personal rulers, has his problems. Most

nagging is the need jealously to guard his authority. No potential challenger is permitted to gain a power base. Mobutu's officials know that their jobs depend solely on the President's discretion. Frequently, he fires cabinet ministers, often without explanation. He appoints loyal army officers and other faithfuls as provincial governors, but only to provinces outside their home areas. And he constantly reshuffles and purges his governors and high army command. Everyone is kept off balance. Everyone must vie for his patronage. Mobutu holds the cards and the game is his.

In this atmosphere of suspicion and intrigue, the chief can become isolated. If he falls into the trap of believing his own propaganda, of uncritically accepting the praises sung by his sycophants, he grows increasingly divorced from reality. His inner circle, pursuing their own ambitions, whisper malicious gossip in the strongman's ear regarding supposed palace conspiracies. Rarely in these conditions does the leader possess the discernment to assess the political situation in a dispassionate and balanced manner. Paranoia and overreaction to alleged intrigues are common characteristics of personal rule.

All strongmen attempt to augment their personal authority by appropriating powerful symbols and rituals. They adopt a variety of honorific titles. Kwame Nkrumah became *Osagyefo* (victor in war) Dr Nkrumah; Sékou Touré was *le Grand Silly* (elephant); Jomo Kenyatta was called *Mzee* (the elder) and *Babu wa Taifa* (father of the nation); Julius Nyerere is, more modestly *Mwalimu* (the teacher). The more erratic or deranged a leader, it seems, the more bizarre the title(s) adopted; President Idi Amin became Field Marshall and C.B.E. (Conqueror of the British Empire), and President Bokassa invested himself as first emperor of the Central African Empire. And then there are the visible symbols of authority: Mobutu Sese-Seko's ornate carved stick, Jomo Kenyatta's fly wisk, Kwame Nkrumah's chiefly stool, Haile Selassie's royal lions, Houphouët-Boigny's sacred crocodiles, and so on.

There are differences as well. Certain personal rulers, such as Jomo Kenyatta, Kenneth Kaunda (Zambia) and Félix Houphouët-Boigny (Ivory Coast), retained considerable personal authority, whereas others, such as Daniel arap Moi and Mobutu, possessed little. Personal stature stemming from leadership in anti-colonial struggles, age and political skill facilitates relatively effective and benign rule. Whereas Kenyatta, Kaunda and Houphouët-Boigny could govern with only occasional recourse to force, Moi and Mobutu – not to mention Amin and Bokassa – depended for their survival increasingly on coercion.

However, to a varying degree all strongmen have constructed and maintained their power through patronage. The proliferation of patron–client relationships is, then, the second characteristic of personal rule.

Patrons at all levels build their followings by providing material benefits and prestigious posts to personally loyal clients. These mercenary linkages proliferate as the strongman, his lieutenants and, sometimes, competing national leaders recruit clients from amongst patrons and brokers at the regional or local level and in nominally modern organizations such as bureaucracies and trade unions. Patron–client relationships may interlink, with patrons at one level becoming the clients of those higher up. In this case, these informal networks of personal alliances may stretch from the capital city to the most distant regions.

The extent of political participation affects the reach of these clientelistic networks. National political leaders have one principal incentive to extend their networks to the grassroots – fairly open competitive party or intra-party electoral contests. If autocracy reigns, only those who number among the politically important will share in the spoils:

top bureaucrats, party officials, local notables, national and regional politicians, military officers and trade union officials. As material pay-offs are restricted to a relatively small circle, force increases concomitantly as the major means of holding an excluded population in line.

Spoils come in basically two forms.[5] First, Big Men can provide their followers with access to the state's resources. 'Jobs for the boys' in the civil service, government boards and public corporations can be furnished by legal or illegal means. They can, perhaps legally but certainly unethically, channel low-interest loans and contracts from public agencies to their friends and allies. Agricultural development corporations, for instance, may draw their resources from levies on peasant production, yet allocate their loans mainly to the rich and powerful. Some patrons will also supply their clients with opportunities for illegal gain from public office; or, at least, they may allow illicit practices to go unpunished for fear of losing support. Corruption is one such opportunity – accepting or extorting bribes for decisions or actions taken in a public capacity. Others include theft of public property, the illegal appropriation of public revenues (fraud) and nepotism.

Secondly, strongmen and/or other Big Men reward their clients by granting preferential access to resources which, though outside the public sector, are subject to governmental regulation or influence. For example, an aspiring businessman is required to obtain a licence to establish a transport company, a taxi service or a distributorship for a certain commodity. He must have a permit to import various items or get foreign exchange from the central bank. Indeed, even to purchase land, he may have to satisfy a land board. All these allocations of nongovernmental benefits can become counters in the game of factional manoeuvre.

Illustrations of these practices are legion. Zaire is, again, an extreme case, this time of corruption and abuse of office.

One study of public administration in this country lists dozens of instances of routine corruption, fraud and theft.[6] Included is the diversion of both US food aid and military assistance (trucks, soft drinks, K-rations) to the black market for the enrichment of top bureaucrats and officers. As the authoritative magazine *Africa Confidential* (3 January 1979) has laconically observed, 'American officials do not seem to warm to Zaire when they see US army trucks being used as taxis in the rice trade.' Mobutu himself has provided the most damning indictment. In a 1977 speech to the Legislative Council, he declared:

In a word, everything is for sale, anything can be bought in our country. And in this flow, he who holds the slightest cover of public authority uses it illegally to acquire money, goods, prestige or to avoid obligations. The right to be recognized by a public servant, to have one's children enrolled in school, to obtain medical care, a diploma, etc. [...] are all subject to this tax which, though invisible, is known and expected by all.[7]

The President, however, apparently condones the practices he publicly condemns – except on the part of those who show excessive greed. In 1976, he warned civil servants that 'if you want to steal, steal a little in a nice way. But if you steal too much to become rich overnight, you'll be caught.'[8] Western sources estimated Mobutu's own fortune in early 1984 at nearly $4 billion, most of it in Swiss banks.[9] This was almost equivalent to Zaire's foreign debt.

Corruption and misuse of public office reach exceptional levels also in Nigeria. As a well-placed permanent secretary in Nigeria's federal service recently commented:

The evil exists in every facet of our society. You bribe to get your child into school; you pay to secure a job and also continue to pay in some cases to retain it; you pay 10 per cent of any contract obtained; you dash [bribe] the tax officer to avoid paying taxes; you pay a hospital doctor or nurse to get proper attention; you pay the policeman to evade arrest. This catalogue of shame can continue without end.

Indeed, public revelations of the spectacular corruption of Nigeria's government, both before and after the August 1983 general elections, helped precipitate the *coup* by Major-General Mohammed Buhari on December 31, 1983.

But, though corruption exists, the participants are not limited to African public officials. A certain hypocrisy is evident in Western reportage on this subject. The fact is that foreign corporations, salesmen and investors are frequently quite willing to offer secret inducements to obtain plush contracts or access to natural resources or protected markets in Africa. And these corporations normally receive a high return on the ten per cent 'commissions' paid to public officials or their agents. Bribery, these foreigners say, is a necessary business practice. However, their willing collusion spreads the malady they so loftily condemn in public.

The other major instrument for establishing and maintaining the strongman's rule is a personally loyal armed force. Owing to weak legitimacy and the constriction of the charmed circle with access to the spoils, rulers must increasingly rely upon the threat or use of coercion for their survival. Thus, the distinction between military and civilian regimes is ultimately misleading. On the one hand, we have army leaders who seize power and 'civilianize' their regimes; on the other hand, we find civilian rulers who feel they must cultivate and co-opt their military commanders. The distinction, then, is really one between the direct and indirect political influence of the armed forces.

Security organs proliferate in the years following independence. Insecure leaders adopt first one tactic and then another in an endless search for stability and order. Presidents recruit their personal bodyguard or palace guard from amongst their own tribesmen or from a foreign country to maximize reliability. For example, President Milton Obote of Uganda still surrounded himself in 1984 with a corps of

20 Tanzanian soldiers. Ghanaian Ft.-Lieutenant Jerry Rawlings, after his successful *coup* against President Limann in December 1981, used a contingent of Libyan soldiers to protect himself. The special battalion that guards President Mobutu is recruited largely from the President's own region; President Amadou Ahidjo of the Cameroon followed the same stratagem. These leaders share a common hope – that foreign mercenaries or personally loyal kinsmen will be immune to domestic plots and conspiracies.

The fate that befell President Biya of the Cameroon shows that no leader can afford to ignore this dictum. Succeeding Amadou Ahidjo, Biya erred by retaining the presidential guard that Ahidjo had recruited mainly from personally loyal northerners. A well-armed force, it nearly succeeded in ousting Biya, a southerner, in a bloody attempted *coup* of April 1984.

Secret police are another instrument of rule. A civilian or military agency, sometimes both, conducts intelligence and surveillance to ferret out conspiracies. Some of those agencies are trained by and receive technical assistance from external patrons, especially France and the Soviet Union. Prior to 1980, France's SDECE (Foreign Information and Counterintelligence Service) was deeply involved in these activities. It assisted such conservative countries as Zaire, Morocco, Central African Republic and Gabon and helped to destabilize such unfriendly regimes as Benin.[10] The American CIA (Central Intelligence Agency) helped Zaire's Mobutu with technical assistance for the presidential bodyguard and security apparatus and made intelligence reports on the machinations of Mobutu's opponents.[11] And the Soviet KGB has played a similar role for such Marxist-Leninist regimes as Ethiopia.

The secret police are, in a few countries, the principal means of maintaining personal rule. The case of Sudan's President Jaafar Nimeiry, an archetypal strongman, provided a clear illustration. After his successful *coup* of 1969, he held all the strings of power; he was the head of state, head of government, leader of the only legal party (the misnamed Sudanese Socialist Party), commander-in-chief of the armed forces and head of the Sudanese news agency. And Nimeiry, who was regularly 're-elected' president with majorities in excess of 99 per cent, made all decisions. One well-informed Sudanese wryly observed that, though the President was surrounded by a coterie of advisers, 'the President's advisers receive more advice than they give'.

Nimeiry maintained his personal following by adhering to an age-old formula – reward the faithful handsomely, and ferociously punish the disloyal. A meticulous man, the President's recipe was finely honed: to each new cabinet minister, the gift of a Mercedes-Benz; to each new general, a Peugeot; and to each new minister at the regional level, a Renault. (It is not clear who received a Volkswagen.) Another example: his erstwhile colleagues on the original Revolutionary Council of 1969 were not dispatched empty-handed when they were removed from office. While taking all the power for himself, he appeased them with a house, a car and a pension each. Later, when three of these comrades dabbled in a *coup* attempt, they were hanged.

There was a lot more to the seamy side of Nimeiry's rule. Repression became his only recourse as he alienated one group of allies after another – from the communist left to the Islamic right – and survived repeated *coup* attempts. His prisons bulged with political prisoners. To travel within Sudan, both foreigners and citizens had to obtain special documents and citizens even had to obtain a special pass to enter the international departures terminal at the Khartoum airport. Police at frequent roadblocks checked identity cards. Fundamentalist Islamic law (sharia) introduced in 1983 provided a further means of intimidation. The premise of 'an eye for an eye' and the brutal public punishments inflicted served to remind dissidents of the regime's power and determination to maintain absolute control.

Plainclothes security men were everywhere. In 1984 well-placed Sudanese estimated that 30,000 operated in Khartoum alone. Each neighbourhood had its own plain-clothesman and each university class was assumed to harbour an informer. Many Sudanese intellectuals can recount tales concerning their harassment by the secret police. One graduate student in sociology, for instance, had her notes confiscated while researching Khartoum's infor-mal sector. A car washer she interviewed was, in fact, a plainclothes policeman who arrested her for 'asking ques-tions without a permit'. And as repression intensified, Nimeiry tried to cover all the bases; his personal jet and pilot were always on stand-by, insurance against the inevitable day of his regime's overthrow. This transpired in April 1985.

The armed forces are generally the strongman's achilles heel. How can he maintain personal control? The political potential of the military is inescapably vivid, especially to many a strongman who himself grabbed power via the army. To capture or neutralize the army, the ruler has two options. He can transform it into a force led and, perhaps, manned by his followers, or he can build up a personally loyal counterforce. But there is a catch. Either route may provoke the officer corps if they perceive a threat to their prestige or professional autonomy.

Sometimes, historical circumstances impede a strong-man's efforts to control the military. Regiments recruited by colonial governments could produce an army at indepen-dence whose officers and men derive from tribes outside those of the governing coalition. This could occur because the British preferred to recruit soldiers from the more backward or 'martial' tribes. The result was an uneasy relationship between the military and rulers when ethnic tensions were high. But an astute president would shrink from thrusting his own ethnic supporters into the upper ranks too quickly; if he alienates the existing military leadership, they may rise against him before he has the armed strength to protect himself. He must be more discreet. Instead, he might cautiously develop or expand a personally loyal paramilitary force in order to checkmate a potentially unreliable army.

Such was Kenyatta's strategy in Kenya. The colonial army inherited by the Kikuyu-led government was overwhelmingly Kamba and Kalenjin in composition. The Kikuyu, Embu and Meru were not welcomed into the colonial army because of their role as guerrillas during the Mau Mau Rebellion of 1952–60. Could Kenyatta depend on this military, led as it was by Wakamba and Kalenjin? These tribes were periodically hostile to his KANU (Kenya African National Union). Evidently he thought not. To dilute this tribal imbalance, he recruited from a number of other groups, all the while cautiously promoting Kikuyus into the upper reaches of the military hierarchy and retaining a British commander-in-chief for many years.

Even more astutely, Kenyatta recognized the potential of a Kikuyuized and expanded GSU – a paramilitary force the British had used so cleverly against African dissidents.[12] He took special care that this General Service Unit was led by highly capable men and equipped with the best weapons. And the GSU acted on the direct orders of Kenyatta and his lieutenants. Its main camp was at Gatundu, strategically located close to the Presidential estate and on a major road that army units would travel in the event of a *coup*. Not only did the GSU provide a checkmate to the army, but it also constituted a handy, awesome force to direct against demonstrators. Periodic GSU sweeps of the University of Nairobi campus were a highly effective means of intimidation, though the beating and raping of students brought protests from parents in high places.

Daniel arap Moi, who assumed the presidency after Kenyatta's death in 1978, faced a number of challenges. But a major test of his political abilities was whether he could control the security apparatus. A Kalenjin, Moi was not consoled by the strength and strategic location of the Kikuyu-dominated GSU. To be secure, he felt, he needed to be free of Kikuyu tutelage. His response was predictable: he promoted certain loyal officers in the army and Special Branch and, on a suitable occasion, he disarmed but did not disband the GSU. His suspicions about discontent amongst the Luo compounded his headaches and were confirmed when the largely Luo and Waluhya airforce attempted to seize power in August 1982. Moi responded by disbanding the Kenyan Air Force. But his situation is still not secure. More than his predecessor, Moi is vulnerable and will remain so as long as he must govern without the support of the two largest and most economically powerful tribes, the Luo and Kikuyu.

Uganda provides an even more vivid illustration of how strongmen and their opponents vie for control of the army. The manipulation of ethnic loyalties has been especially important in these contests.[13]

Prime Minister Milton Obote occupied an unenviably weak position at independence in 1962. He and his UPC (Uganda Peoples' Congress) were confronted with particularly deep ethnic schisms. The Baganda, the wealthiest and most numerous tribe, pined after their own state. To mollify them, the independence constitution instituted a peculiar federalism with Buganda in the privileged position of a 'state within a state'. Of course, this special status exacerbated jealousies between Buganda and the five smaller Bantu kingdoms of the South. At the same time, the more economically and educationally disadvantaged northerners (35 per cent of the population) feared domination by the Southerners, in general, and the Baganda, in particular. The predominance of Waganda in the top echelons of the federal civil service fed this fear. To complicate the situation, the north was itself divided: the Nilotes (mainly the Langi, Obote's tribe and the Acholi) comprised 14 per cent of the population, the Nilo-Hamites of the North-east, 12 per cent and the 'Sudanic' peoples of the West Nile, five per cent. These northerners formed the popular base of the UPC. With only 43 of the 87 seats in the National Assembly and not a single one in Buganda, Obote had to forge a coalition with the traditional Baganda Party, the Kebaka Yekka (KY). This was an inherently unstable alliance.

Obote held one trump, though. The British had unwittingly created a favourable situation which he could manipulate to his advantage. The colonial government had recruited the Fourth (Ugandan) Battalion of the King's African Rifles from amongst northerners, especially the Langi and Acholi; these tribes were considered to be more reliable and 'warlike' than the sophisticated southerners. This battalion constituted the core of the new Ugandan army. Obote and his lieutenants seized the opportunity to use this army as a power base by continuing to recruit a disproportionate number of soldiers from the Nilotes. Ironically, nature had provided him with a splendid physical rationalization – the southerners generally failed to measure up to the minimum height and chest measurement established by the British recruiters. In January 1964, Obote, in concert with General Idi Amin from the West Nile, extended this policy by inducting Sudanese refugees in northern Uganda into the army as politically reliable soldiers.

What united the army was the northerners' hostility toward the Baganda. Reacting to the tension, the Bagandan leaders further exacerbated hostilities by establishing an unofficial self-defence force, armed men wearing local government police uniforms. In light of the deteriorating relations with the Baganda and the KY, Obote executed a *coup* against Buganda in February 1966 by unilaterally trans- forming Uganda into a unitary state with centralized power in his hands alone. This step led in May to a clash between the Ugandan army and the Kebaka's palace guard. Defeat- ed, the Baganda were thereafter treated as a conquered people.

So much for the cohesion of the army. With the defeat of Buganda, various northern politicians tried to promote their factional interests by forging links with their brethren in the officer corps. Obote, struggling to maintain control, promoted personally loyal army officers and created a Langi-dominated paramilitary General Service Department which his cousin commanded. By the late 1960s, the main axis of competition within the army was between Obote and the army commander, General Amin. Obote took the offensive in September 1970 with a massive reorganization that placed his followers (mainly Acholis and Langis) in 20 key army posts.

But Amin was craftier than anticipated. He out- manoeuvred the President by transferring 22 of his West Nile and Nubian allies to command posts in the strategic Malire Regiment on the outskirts of Kampala. His stage was perfectly set. On the day of Amin's *coup* in January 1972, 32 of this mechanized unit's 43 officers were Nubians, Kakwe and Lugbara (the latter two from Amin's West Nile). As history records, the Malire Regiment won the day and Obote went into exile.[14]

Brutality and large-scale violence followed. Amin exter- minated officers and men of Langi and Acholi origins. The dictator made the army his personal machine with officers and men linked to the new strongman by both ethnic and mercenary ties. Common soldiers prospered from thefts and extortions that went unpunished. Army officers grew rich by controlling the smuggling of coffee into Kenya and the illegal import of manufactured goods. Amin further assured their personal loyalty by turning over to his followers the assets of expelled Asians in 1972–3. In return, the army, helped by the secret police in the so-called Bureau of State Research, terrorized and murdered potential dissidents.

An election in 1980 returned Obote and the UPC to power some months after the Tanzanian army's ousting of Amin. But the established pattern of government–army relations did not change. In a chaotic political situation, Obote felt he could depend only upon his Langi tribe. Currently, the Langi predominates in both the officer corps and the army's rank and file. So cautious is President Obote now that even the closely related Acholi have little chance for senior military positions.[15] And Obote has only a tenuous grip on the Ugandan army whose soldiers still engage in illegal and predatory activities to supplement their inadequate salaries.

Foreign protectors also buttress the repressive capacity of some strongmen. Africa's internal disarray encourages imperialist countries to intervene, overtly or covertly, in political life to encourage friends or unseat or punish enemies. But in the process, external patrons promote governmental irresponsibility, oppressiveness and venality.

The Soviet Union, France, the United States and Libya are the principal interventionist powers, but South Africa, Britain and Belgium have also been involved. Motives are various. Power and influence are the usual reasons for superpower involvement; Africa becomes just one more pawn in the global East–West conflict. Others, such as Libya and South Africa, strive to advance their regional geopolitical interests. And France, Britain and Belgium want to safeguard large investments or vital sources of raw materials. France also asserts a claim to global influence by maintaining a powerful military, economic and cultural presence in West and Central Africa.

Foreign intervention in Africa's domestic politics takes four basic forms. One is transfer of arms to friendly regimes. Between 1973 and 1978, the value of weapons sold or donated to the continent of Africa increased ten-fold, from $US 300 million to over $US 3 billion annually. The Soviet Union was the most bountiful arms supplier accounting for about one-half the total, followed by France (25 per cent) and the US (13 per cent).[16] Most weaponry was the type needed for external defense – advanced jet fighters, tanks, armoured personnel carriers and so on. But, in addition, certain foreign powers augmented the capacity of their favoured regimes in the area of counterinsurgency and repression. Evidently, they hoped that client regimes would be able to suppress dissidence before it flared into open insurrection. This would relieve the patron power from the unpopular role of direct military intervention against guerrilla movements.

Especially popular in the area of repression technology is crowd control equipment – tear gas, MACE, batons, shields and helmets, and small arms and ammunition. Also welcome are light aircraft, troop carrying helicopters and armoured cars. France and United States have provided Zaire with the Cessna F337, armed with machine guns and bombs, rockets or napalm canisters; Chad, Mauritania and Zimbabwe have similar supplies. Most highly prized is the Cadillac Gage V-150 Commando armoured car which is effective against both urban rioters and rural insurgents.

Recently, some new suppliers have entered the international market. Italy has provided Libya, Ghana, Tunisia, Somalia, South Africa, Morocco and Zambia with aircraft and helicopters. Brazil and Israel, the former with a well-earned reputation in the repression business, have broken into the African market with aircraft and armoured cars.[17] Having long been a supplier of weaponry to South Africa, Israel is expanding into Black Africa with the reopening of diplomatic relations with a number of African countries.

A second form of foreign military intervention is the use of surrogate forces to quell insurrections against friendly regimes. Large powers, whether the Soviet Union, the United States or France, prefer not to commit their own troops in Africa. Such actions are costly in terms of unpopularity at home and one's image as an imperialist abroad. But for a foreign patron to supply, train and transport the troops of a Third-World ally is perceived in a different light; these surrogate troops can then intervene on behalf of the foreign patron in an African conflict.

Numerous examples of this pattern come to mind. The USSR has, of course, used Cuban troops in this capacity in Angola and Ethiopia since 1975. In the early eighties, about 35,000 Cuban troops were still in Africa. For their part, the Western powers put together an inter-African surrogate force in the late 1970s composed of Moroccans, and small contingents from Senegal, Togo, and the Ivory Coast. The Moroccans saw action in Zaire in 1977–8. More recently, Zaire has shown itself a willing client of the French and Americans; Mobutu dispatched 2,000 troops to Chad in 1983 to counter the pro-Libyan insurgents.

Occasionally, though, foreign powers do commit expeditionary forces to assist African friends. This is the third and most direct form of intervention. France has been most willing to directly commit troops.[18] Defence agreements link France with a core of neocolonies: Senegal, Ivory Coast, Gabon, Central African Republic, Djibouti, Togo and Cameroon. These arrangements involve base agreements and African participation in occasional joint war games and dramatically illustrate to the world France's support for incumbent regimes. France and Zaire have been bound by a similar agreement since 1977. And France still has Military Technical Assistance Agreements with all former French colonies (except Guinea), and Rwanda and Burundi as well.

Since 1960, France's strategic involvement has changed its form. It has reduced its military presence, but augmented its capacity for rapid military intervention in Africa. In 1960, there were about 60,000 French troops in more than 90 garrisons in tropical Africa, including Madagascar; by 1981, the force had declined to one-tenth that number in only six countries. However, these withdrawals were more than matched by the expansion of an airborne rapid deployment force (RDF) stationed at home. This home-based force has a distinct advantage; it minimizes the risk to France of being labelled an imperialist power in Africa. The French military presence is maintained by transit, refueling and support facilities for the RDF and scattered military advisory teams and small troop contingents in allied countries.

France's forces are active; they have participated in African conflicts far more frequently than the soldiers of any other country. Many a strongman's regime owed thanks to France in the 1960s when it suppressed riots and uprisings. And under the direction of President Giscard d'Estaing there was a fresh spate of interventions in the late seventies. Table 7 records the remarkable number and variety of France's direct military action in Black Africa.

Other Western powers have been much more reticent to send in expeditionary forces. Britain's last intervention was in late 1964 when it suppressed military mutinies in Tanzania, Kenya and Uganda. Kenya remains just about the only subsaharan country in which Britain still plays a military role of significance. It supplies training facilities and a few hundred British troops who are stationed inconspicuously at Nyeri, 120 miles north of Nairobi. Together with the American marines in Mombasa, the British presence doubtless stabilizes President Moi's rule.

The United States seems to regard Black Africa's security concerns as primarily the responsibility of its European

Table 7. *French military intervention in tropical Africa*

Country	Year	Reason for intervention
Cameroon	1959–64	Counterrevolutionary war
Senegal	1959–60, 1962	Support for President Senghor during dissolution of Mali Federation and attempted *coup* by Mamadou Dia
Congo	1960, 1962	Suppression of riots
Gabon	1960, 1962 1964	Suppression of riots and uprisings Reversal of *coup* vs. President M'ba
Chad	1960–3 1968–75 } 1977–80 } 1983–4	Suppression of riots and uprisings War vs. FROLINAT War vs. Goukouni Woddeye
Mauritania	1961 1977–8	Suppression of riots Air support vs. POLISARIO in former Spanish Sahara
Niger	1973	Prevention of military mutiny/*coup*
Djibouti	1976–7	Operation against Somali irredentism
Zaire	1977, 1978	Suppression of Shaba rebellions
Central African Republic	1979	French supported *coup* vs. Emperor Bokassa I

Source: R. Luckham, 'French Militarism in Africa', *ROAPE*, 24 (1982), 61.

allies. It has given logistical support to French, Belgian and Moroccan expeditionary forces, supplying, for example, air support for the interventions in Shaba, Zaire in the late seventies and Chad in 1983. And the Carter administration, seeking bases to protect US interests in the Persian Gulf through its prospective rapid deployment force, established itself in Mombasa, Berbera (Somalia) and off the coast of Oman. By 1983, the force numbered 220,000, and Reagan planned to double its complement of paratroopers and marines.

Along with this military build-up went a new US concern for the stability of neighbouring countries subject to Libyan machinations, including the Sudan and Chad. There is a real danger that a US president may be tempted to react to instability in one of these countries by committing troops to aid the ruling oligarchy. Once in, these forces could not easily be extricated.

Africa's more powerful countries also advance regional ambitions by taking advantage of their weaker neighbours. Qaddafy – the 'madman of Tripoli' according to Anwar Sadat – is apparently aiming to construct an Islamic empire in Black Africa; the Libyan leader has provided support to client groups in Chad, Mali, Niger, and Uganda. And South Africa does what it can to control its neighbours. To destabilize hostile regimes in Angola, Mozambique and Zimbabwe, South Africa supplied guerrilla movements and executed lightning land and air attacks on strategic targets. The aim is to force incumbent regimes to expel or control South African and Namibian exiles who are committed to the overthrow of the white regime, an aim largely achieved with South Africa's signing of non-aggression pacts with Mozambique and Angola in 1984. Foreign sponsored civil wars can profoundly affect precarious governments. The economies of Mozambique and Angola, already tottering from severe droughts and other problems, were brought to the point of collapse by 1983–4.

Covert political action by intelligence agencies on behalf of African allies is the final form of foreign intervention. The SDECE, the French intelligence agency, has already been mentioned. It is still well entrenched in French-speaking Africa, though it no longer enjoys the free hand it possessed under President d'Estaing. As for the Soviet Union's KGB, little is known about its covert action in Africa. But the activities of the CIA are quite well documented.

The CIA has defined its interests fairly clearly. It has recognized that most of French-speaking Africa is the SDECE's territory, focussing American covert activities on Zaire and Angola. Zaire's importance stems from the large US investment of over one billion dollars, its strategic location in central Africa and its mineral deposits. Angola, on the other hand, attracted American attention during its lengthy struggle against the Portuguese masters. The CIA supported the pro-Western FNLA (National Front for the Liberation of Angola) and UNITA (National Union for the Total Liberation of Angola) against the Marxist MPLA (Popular Movement for the Liberation of Angola). Nonetheless, with Soviet and Cuban assistance, the MPLA established a tenuous control of Angola in 1976.

The CIA's range of activities in Central Africa has been extraordinary. These have included:

subsidization of political leaders and parties, military and internal security functionaries and *coup*-makers; political assassination plots; technical assistance for a presidential bodyguard and security apparatus; provision of a third country foreign military combat and combat support personnel; supply of arms and related equipment.[19]

If one considers the case of just Zaire, the scope of American intelligence activities is dramatically illustrated. The CIA planned the assassination of Premier Patrice Lumumba in 1961. It facilitated the emergence of General Mobutu as strongman in the period between 1960 and 1964. In 1964, it mounted a clandestine paramilitary operation to defeat a rebellion. And it further reinforced Mobutu's regime by providing the president with training and intelligence reports and organizing the capture of his opponent, Moise Tshombe, as his plane flew over Algeria. The CIA tried to coordinate these covert acts with public Western activities in central Africa, including in particular, conventional economic and military assistance.

This new imperialism has important implications for African political life. To advance geopolitical goals, seek glory and safeguard investments, foreign patrons supply cooperative African leaders with just about anything they need to stay in or win power. This outside political support magnifies the seamy characteristics of personal rule – the authoritarianism, the recourse to repression, the rampant factionalism, venality and instability.

The weak legitimacy of African governments is further undermined by the manifest and abject dependence of various strongmen upon foreign patrons who play the tune to which these leaders dance. Neither reform nor popular change of a regime is attainable if foreign powers manipulate events to suit corrupt and despotic leaders. Clandestine campaigns to replace rulers who incur the displeasure of the imperialists ignite factional and violent conflict, exacerbate political instability and corrupt new layers of aspirant politicians. Capitalism thus assumes a particularly repressive and unstable cast in Africa and the masses sink deeper into cynicism and despair.

In sum, African tendencies toward a personalization of power are rooted in history and a particular social structure. But the oppressiveness and corruption often associated with this are not wholly explicable by reference to factors internal to each country. Western governments, in particular, share a responsibility.

The effect of internal disarray and foreign interference, combined with world recession, is the downward spiral of political and economic decline, to which we now turn.

❧ 6 ❧

THE DOWNWARD SPIRAL

Downward spiral – Ghanaians, Nigerians, Zairois, Zambians, Sudanese, Tanzanians, Kenyans, Ugandans may not describe their predicament in this way. Yet they are brutally familiar with the phenomenon to which the term refers. State decay, economic decline and the rise of the black market are the prime features. They are, moreover, intimately interrelated.

Zaire, once again, provides a dramatic example.[1] The decline of the state since independence, manifest in enormous corruption, maladministration, arbitrary use of authority and deterioration of public services, produced unconducive conditions for economic growth. By 1980, the state resembled nothing more than an organization of profiteers whose sole shared goal was the use of public office for personal enrichment. While Mobutu's clique reaped rich harvests and invested millions of dollars in secure countries abroad, the modern economy languished. Large-scale capitalist firms could prosper only where they were able to profit from monopoly conditions or exploit mineral reserves within carefully protected enclaves. Agriculture, the livelihood of the vast majority, increasingly reverted to subsistence.

In desperation, those excluded from the charmed political circle turned to the parallel economy. Enormous price inflation in relation to wages and the unavailabiltiy of many goods at controlled prices meant that workers could not feed, house and clothe their families. To survive, black marketing was essential. The informal economy thus boomed in the 1970s despite the state. By 1976, more than half of the household income of employed urban dwellers in Western Zaire derived from informal economic activities. Ironically, certain entrepreneurs in the informal sector grew so rich that even political insiders were attracted to these new economic opportunities lying outside the government's purview. Because the state could neither collect taxes from these unregulated transactions nor prevent fraudulent and corrupt practices, it lost as much as 60 per cent of its potential revenues.[2] Political decline thus begot economic deterioration and vice versa.

What processes generate this downward spiral? In particular, what part is played by personal rule?

Personal rule is potentially highly destructive. It operates, as we have shown, according to a certain logic. To motivate compliance, rulers with meagre legitimacy must fall back on personal loyalties stemming from friendship, kinship, ethnicity and material rewards, or on force or the threat of force. The centrality of mercenary incentives compels factional leaders to manoeuvre for access to new resources with which to maintain or enlarge their following. Politics in the absence of hegemony can thus come to involve only one real issue – who will win office and cut the pie? Every other consideration is secondary.

This environment fosters the decay of state institutions. Political institutions such as the presidency, the parliament, the party, even the judiciary, lose whatever public esteem they commanded. People begin to scoff at the pious utterances of politicians concerning unity, hard work and sacrifice. Bureaucratic institutions also become ineffective and lose their technical rationality. Nepotism and patronage swell the bureaucratic ranks with incompetents and time-servers. Those civil servants who are competent and honest are demoralized by the graft, fraud and theft of public property. Indiscipline and lassitude paralyse the bureaucratic apparatus.

Political decay feeds on itself. As consent declines, politicians rely more heavily on pay-offs and force. Dissidents, in turn, employ violent tactics to obtain ideological or sectional goals. A rising incidence of crime, riots, rebellions, civil wars or *coups* signals acute political instability. As citizens grow accustomed to bribing officials in even routine matters, corruption becomes the norm.

Political instability, one major indicator of state decay, is endemic in Africa. Indeed, personal rule is inherently unstable. The stakes of political competition are high, while the rules of the political game are nebulous in a system characterized by ethnic, regional or religious schisms and an absence of established political traditions. A strongman must possess superb political skills or strong support from an external power to maintain an orderly political life.

If we define as politically unstable those countries that experience two or more episodes of political violence (revolution, rebellion, *coup*, insurrection) within a decade, then the majority of neopatrimonial countries are unstable. Indeed, by mid 1984, the 46 independent countries of tropical Africa had suffered at least 60 successful *coups* alone. Ghana and Benin topped the list, each having suffered five successful overthrows. Nigeria experienced four such unconstitutional changes of regime. Uganda's people have been tormented by virtually all forms of political violence since 1972. And even those African paragons of political stability, Kenya and Cameroon, had to quash bloody attempted overthrows in August 1982 and April 1984 respectively. (Some say that perhaps Kenya's vaunted stability has been exaggerated; after all, three major politicians were assassinated in the first dozen years of independence.) Rarely in Africa does one observe peaceful and constitutional succession to the presidency. In the period 1960–82, there were only six instances.[3]

The citizens of a third of tropical Africa's countries share the worst of all possible political worlds – instability combined with severe oppression. Defenceless before the depredations of an undisciplined army or governing party, the people of Uganda, Zaire and Equatorial Guinea live in unceasing fear and turmoil. Military indiscipline is a real problem for all regimes that depend on force to survive. The central government retains only a tenuous grip over military, paramilitary or police units even in such countries as Ghana, Nigeria and Kenya. Personal security is endangered not only by the criminal elements, but also by the 'forces of order'.

Civil strife, together with famine, have driven millions of Africans into exile. In 1981, half of the world's refugee population originated from subsaharan Africa. Countries harbouring large refugee populations, especially Somalia, compounded their economic problems, even with United Nations' assistance. One country's political violence can indirectly blight its neighbours' economic prospects.

A second indicator of state decay is a deterioration of administrative capacity. This, too, is a phenomenon closely linked to neopatrimonialism.

Max Weber believed that only bureaucracy could provide modern capitalism with what it required – efficient, specialized, rational (i.e., non-arbitrary) administration. He conceived of bureaucratic organization as an ideal type possessing certain characteristics:

(1) the definition of a fixed jurisdiction for each public office;
(2) the arrangement of those offices in hierarchical order;

(3) the appointment and promotion of employees on the grounds of technical competence and training;

(4) the separation of public office from the officeholder's private or business activities; and

(5) the treatment of employment in an office as a full time, permanent job[4]

Most African administrations diverge so widely from this model that the application of the term bureaucracy is quite misleading.

Why did this deterioration occur? One must adopt an historical perspective to answer this question. In Western Europe, the transition from patrimonial administration to bureaucracy took two to three centuries. Gradually, the administrative offices were separated from the royal households and personal considerations in administration were replaced by impersonal, universalistic criteria. Africa has not had this opportunity for gradual adaptation; instead, as one Nigerian commentator noted, there was 'premature bureaucratization'.[5]

Africa's bureaucracies were established at the end of the nineteenth and the beginning of the twentieth centuries, and under alien auspices. In most colonies, Europeans staffed the upper echelons of bureaucracies until the era of postwar decolonization. (Senegal was a major exception; here, assimilated *évolués* participated in administration from an early stage.) Africans were mainly relegated to the clerical and manual grades and to the running of various forms of local government. But these institutions had restricted powers and, in any event, operated under the supervision of a field officer of the central government; in British colonies, he was the District Officer. Indirect rule in the British territories rarely devolved substantial authority to traditional African rulers. In practice, only assimilated Africans – those with European education and life-style (including language, clothing, manners, even religion) – could work in the technical and administrative grades of colonial bureaucracy. Bureaucratic employment was, therefore, regarded as *olu oyibo* ('white man's job' in Ibo). This alien flavour persisted even after the barriers to African employment and promotion came tumbling down with the dawn of independence.

The fact that African administrations diverge from the model of bureaucracy, some explain with reference to traditional norms. This is an oversimplification. Were traditional cultures all uniformly antagonistic to modern organizational forms? These cultures were in fact quite diverse. Certain African societies were governed by hierarchical, patrimonial administrative systems akin to those of medieval Europe. Why then were the administrative norms of northern Nigeria, Ethiopia, Ashanti or Buganda not adaptable to modern bureaucracy? Surely the traditional norms of corporate solidarity could have been expanded to encompass the notion of impartiality in the service of the nation rather than the kinship group.

The point is, of course, there was no *time* for such adaptations. Crash Africanization programmes in the 1950s and sixties propelled Africans into high bureaucratic office. Only a few leaders such as Houphouët-Boigny in the Ivory Coast and Hastings Banda in Malawi resisted pressures to replace white civil servants with hastily promoted countrymen.

With independence, weakly institutionalized bureaucratic norms often quickly gave way in the face of political pressures. 'Having succeeded in driving away the colonial masters, the victors fell back to distribute their booty.'[6] A major aspect of the spoils was employment in the bureaucracy. As patrons manoeuvred, ethnic and/or factional affiliation tended to replace technical competence in hiring and promotion, and nepotism and corruption to replace impartiality in the exercise of authority. Although many competent civil servants resist these trends, theirs is a difficult struggle. They can rarely appeal to constitutional restraints upon the political rulers' powers, for these are neither recognized nor enforced. A deeper problem is the absence of a hegemonic class, discussed in Chapter 4, with sufficient power and independence to force coherence and discipline upon the state apparatus. Consequently, the administrative system adapts to the exigencies of neopatrimonial rule at the cost of its bureaucratic characteristics.

The outstanding danger is, of course, that the abuse of office will become uncontrollable. Unrestrained corruption can pervade the civil service, statutory boards and public corporations; what begins as occasional acts of public misconduct, such as occur in all bureaucracies, spreads like a cancer. The result is a pathological condition of 'systemic corruption' – an administration in which 'wrong-doing has become the norm', whereas the 'notion of public responsibility has become the exception, not the rule'. Corruption is then 'so regularized and institutionalized that organizational supports back wrong-doing and actually penalize those who live up to the old norms'.[7]

So deeply engrained does this pattern become that it is difficult to eradicate. In Ghana, for instance, commissions of inquiry into official wrong-doing have accompanied each new regime (1966, 1972, 1979, 1982) and each set of commissions unearthed, not unexpectedly, massive corruption and graft. Every commission recommended stiffer penalties and/or special police agencies to ferret out these practices. Yet the situation has gone from bad to worse – until, in 1983, Flight-Lieutenant Jerry Rawlings, the new ruler, took the drastic step of shooting people found guilty of major acts of corruption.

In Nigeria, too, there are periodic clean-up campaigns, usually instigated by a *coup d'état*. There has been an

Operation-Purge-the-Nation, an Ethical Revolution, the establishment of a Permanent Corrupt Practices Investigation Bureau, the institution of Codes of Ethics for public officials, the sacking of some prominent (or usually less prominent) offenders. And for a brief time, public servants are cautious; but then the campaign peters out and systemic corruption recurs.

Decay of political and administrative institutions in a system of personal rule is not, however, inevitable. A leader with exceptional political skills and a long-sighted strategy can contain the destructive aspects of neopatrimonialism. The Ivory Coast is a case in point.

President Houphouët-Boigny is the archetypal personal ruler. As two French observers note, 'In practice, the Ivorian state and its chief are almost indistinguishable. He is the source of the launching, the conception and the regulation of the Ivorian experience.'[8] All important decisions and appointments are made by him.

Like all strongmen, Houphouët-Boigny governs by the manipulation of patron–client linkages and control of a coercive apparatus. His rule is, however, special because of certain unique touches. First, he disposes of considerable personal authority. This derives from his domination of the political scene since the Second World War and his leadership of the anticolonial struggle (such as it was). Opposition elements who might wish to displace *le vieux* (the old man) are hard-pressed to find supporters. In the second place, the President adeptly defuses or neutralizes dissent without recourse to brute force. Adopting a monarchical style, Houphouët-Boigny periodically invites the leaders of aggrieved groups to address him with their grievances. *Le dialogue*, as he calls it, defuses political crises by permitting potentially disruptive groups such as civil servants, teachers, the unemployed and trade unionists to feel they matter, they have been heard. Later, the President responds to their complaints in whole or in part. His technique is to reduce grievances to something tangible – money. If teachers are restless, give them a pay hike. If civil servants feel aggrieved, give them access to housing loans. To date, this strategy has been effective.

Another distinctive feature is Houphouët-Boigny's ability to call on French military support in the event of civil strife. The 800–900 French troops stationed at Port Bouët, which is strategically located next to the international airport, deter the rebellious. With the development of its rapid deployment force, the French can mount a major military intervention within hours, and their defence pact with the Ivory Coast would justify such action. All these factors illuminate the basis of the Ivory Coast's exceptional political stability and peacefulness.

The Ivorian civil service is an effective institution and this is because Houphouët-Boigny has shielded it from the corrosive effects of personal rule. True, the President and his lieutenants distribute patronage to maintain political loyalties. Personal followers are rewarded with jobs in parastatals, land on which to build a house in the cities and the registration of children in elite schools.[9] Some resources have, therefore, been wasted. And official corruption is not unheard of in the Ivory Coast, though this is an occasional, not a universal phenomenon. The ruling elite has, therefore, responded to the political exigencies of their society in a familiar manner.

Yet the system is firmly within its creator's control. Despite periodic complaints about the management of public corporations and public utilities, the bureaucracy is relatively competent. This may be partly attributed to Houphouët-Boigny's apparent conviction that bureaucracies, as foreign imports, are best operated by the foreigners, or by Ivorians who have served a lengthy apprenticeship. Until late in the day, the President overrode pressures for a speedy Africanization of the private and public sectors. And even after the promulgation of an Ivorianization policy in 1977, Africanization was slow. In 1980, fully 20 years after independence, only 13 per cent of the directors and one-third of the executives in private companies were Ivorian. Many top positions were still filled with the 40,000 French residents who also were employed in the upper reaches of the civil service and parastatals.[10] Thus, the President continues to insist that (nonpatronage) employees must prove their competence before they can be promoted. The bureaucracy has been insulated to some extent from the game of factional manoeuvre.

The Ivorian experience is not the norm. Elsewhere, as we have discussed, the decay of political and administrative institutions obtains. This decay, compounded by the catastrophic effects of the world recession, brings severe economic problems.

Capitalism flourishes only within the context of the political, legal and economic conditions that we enumerated in Chapter 2. As patrimonial states decay, they become less and less capable of providing this fertile climate. Economic rationality is progressively subverted. Capitalism cannot but remain stunted in this environment. Indeed, in extreme cases, a parasitical and chaotic state pushes the modern economy close to collapse.

Consider first the typical operation of the tax system. To flourish, a capitalist state must match its fiscal policy to the requirements of economic growth. Only a rising output will open up new sources of revenue. Taxes which are too heavy will deter production, blocking the expansion of a government's fiscal base. This is what has often happened in tropical Africa. Massive tax evasion by the rich and counter-productive policies have placed an inordinate tax burden on smallholders. This has discouraged agricultural production, with detrimental consequences for the economy.

Direct taxation, levies on company profits and the income of individuals, is one source of governmental revenue. In the early 1970s, however, direct taxation produced only about one-fifth of the total receipts in African countries as a whole, though there was considerable variance.[11] One factor which accounts for this low proportion is the considerable concessions used to woo direct foreign investment. Another is tax evasion in a system that keeps abysmal financial records and harbours corrupt tax inspectors.

Reliable statistics on the dimensions of the tax evasion are scarce, of course. Although Nigeria may be an extreme case, one well-informed source estimated that tax avoidance reduces his country's personal income tax receipts by as much as 80 to 90 per cent.[12] This accords with a finding that half of those who ought to have paid income taxes in Ibadan in 1958–9 evaded tax payment altogether.[13] Obviously, tax avoidance on this scale shifts the burden to others and leads to deficit budgets and borrowing at home and abroad which only serves to fuel an inflationary spiral.

Indirect taxation, including customs duties, excise and sales tax and levies on agricultural produce, must provide the bulk of revenues. Governments welcome the ease with which these taxes are collected. Also, they are politically acceptable as they place a proportionately greater levy on the politically weak peasants and workers than on the wealthy and powerful elite. But this can backfire, discouraging production amongst the peasants.

Monopsonistic marketing boards are a favoured means of extracting revenues from smallholders. The ostensible aim is to stabilize the price paid to cash-crop producers and eliminate exploitative middlemen. In principle, these boards should accumulate surpluses when world prices are high in order to subsidize producers when prices fall. But practice tells a different story. The boards tend to use their monopoly to keep producer prices artificially low and thereby generate government revenue.

The consequences can be catastrophic. The rural–urban terms of trade turn against the peasants: that is to say, the farmers' income shrinks in relation to the price of items they purchase from the city. At a certain point, this decline in returns to agriculture discourages production and reduces marketed agricultural output. This, in turn, lowers government revenues and earnings of foreign exchange through exports, and raises the import bill as foreign food sources replace local ones. When permitted to continue, this cycle hastens the pace of the downward spiral.

This practice has not passed unnoticed. Fierce condemnation by the International Monetary Fund, the World Bank and other concerned parties has recently effected a return to more reasonable agricultural pricing. But in such countries as Ghana and Uganda, raising agricultural production is still an uphill task. Inappropriate pricing policies are only part of the problem; other hindrances include an inability on the part of marketing boards to organize the prompt collection, storage and marketing of perishable crops and the unavailability to farmers of agricultural inputs and consumer goods at affordable prices. These shortcomings reflect in part the unproductive use to which revenues extracted from the peasants and others are put.

The usual story is that the state soaks up scarce resources, but fails to fulfil its role of facilitating economic growth. First, a swelling public sector rarely means that the government becomes more adept at creating political order. Indeed, we have suggested that political instability is inherent in personal rule. Disorder thus constitutes a major impediment to investment by foreigners and citizens alike. Secondly, an expansion of the public sector rarely creates more effective economic regulation, delivery of essential services or public investment programmes.

Parastatal organizations, in particular, have proliferated

since independence. In many countries, parastatals tripled in the first decade or so after independence; even such market-oriented countries as Kenya and the Ivory Coast participated in this trend. (The public share of Ivorian manufacturing investment, for example, rose dramatically from nil in 1960 to 53 per cent in 1980.) Statutory boards and corporations in all countries run public utilities and social services. There are usually also public enterprises involved in commerce, mining and/or manufacturing, often in the form of joint ventures with private capital. Generally, the government owns 51 per cent of the equity, but cedes management rights to a partner such as a transnational corporation.

Kenya, a less economically nationalist country than many others, exemplifies the diversity of the parastatal sector. In 1980, statutory boards and corporations operated all the conventional public utilities (telephones, electricity, water, ports, etc.) as well as transport services (for instance, Kenya Airways and Kenya Railway Corporation). Public corporations were also engaged in productive activities – agriculture (Kenya Meat Commission, Kenya Co-operative Creameries, National Cereals and Produce Board), finance (Agricultural Finance Corporation), commerce (Kenya National Trading Corporation) and industry (Industrial and Commercial Development Corporation). The government also participated in an array of joint ventures with foreign and local firms, especially in industrial undertakings. And Kenya's public sector accounted for only about 40 per cent of capital formation; in such other countries as Tanzania and Zambia, the proportion was closer to three-quarters in the 1970s.[14]

How have these parastatals fared? Disastrously, on the whole. Public utilities and departments of the civil service have been unable to deliver essential services in many countries. In the 1980s, it was not uncommon to find roads, railways and ports in considerable disrepair. Electricity and water were periodically interrupted. Telephone systems operated haphazardly. Trash removal degenerated, save in the wealthy neighbourhoods. At public schools, students went without supplies and at universities and technical institutes, facilities deteriorated. And hospitals and clinics tried to operate without crucial medicines and equipment. All this chaos created havoc for the production plans of private business, not to mention the productivity of employees.

The record of public enterprises in the productive sector is also generally abysmal. Most often parastatals drained the treasury. The measured and tactful words of the World Bank's 1981 report, *Accelerated Development in Sub-Saharan Africa* (p. 415) provides a temperate account of a common criticism:

> They do not pay taxes. Most of their investment costs are covered by transfers (from government budgets, the banks or marketing organization surpluses); in some cases their cash surplus is less than their depreciation; and in a few instances cash flow does not even cover running costs. A number of the manufacturing parastatals – the mixed public-private enterprises – are moderately profitable. But this is usually because they enjoy very high levels of protection from the world market.

Of course, the picture is not uniformly gloomy. The Ivory Coast, for example, has been praised for efficient administration. But even here many *sociétés d'état* had fallen into disrepute by the mid 1970s; waste and arbitrary and incompetent management were widely alleged. In 1977, Houphouët-Boigny tackled the problem, appointing a cabinet minister specifically to remedy the situation – apparently with some success.[15] True, the publicly owned electricity company provided only an erratic power supply to Abidjan in 1982–3, but this was a consequence of a severe drought that forced hydroelectric power units to shut down.

It is not difficult to account for the shortcomings of the public sector. One factor is clearly the world economic recession. The consequent shortage of foreign exchange means that neither public utilities nor state-controlled enterprises can purchase the imports of equipment, spare parts, and materials they need. Severe climatic conditions also created problems for some parastatals. But beyond this lies the mismanagement that is so intimately related to the decay of the neopatrimonial state.

A well-placed Nigerian administrator has vividly identified the connections between personal rule and public maladministration. His first major complaint is the politicians' penchant for placing their followers in public bodies. Recruitment on a patronage basis allegedly occurs even when the Statutory Corporations Service Commission is formally responsible for selecting personnel. Thus, unsuitable political insiders fill top positions. '[T]hese organizations are [...] overstaffed with redundant personnel who have no other reason for being there than they must be maintained by someone at the expense of these public enterprises.' A second shortcoming is the granting of special consideration to certain clients: '[T]he strong grip of favouritism [...] allows practically all the staff of these enterprises, who have control over the revenue generating sources [...] to grossly undercharge their friends and relations who use the services.' As this theft occurs with respect to electricity, railways, ports and airways, the state loses millions of naira each day. Thirdly, financial control in many public corporations is so tenuous that 'unscrupulous staff members have diverted assets [...] to their private use without being found out'. Because of these practices, the accounts of many boards and public enterprises cannot be reconciled, year after year.[16]

The Rural Electricity Board of Nigeria is an apt case in point. Officials in the 1970s engaged in a whole range of malpractices, according to a commission of inquiry in 1975. They acquired privileged access to electricity for their own private concerns. They extracted kickbacks from equipment suppliers. They consolidated their patron–client networks by the preferential allocation of electricity supplies to individuals, firms and communities who were political supporters. And some of the top officers channelled board revenues to their own enterprises and acquisitions. Indeed, a popular state governor used illegally acquired funds from the Board to buy no fewer than 22 farms and several retail businesses.[17]

Examples could be multiplied to show a similar situation in other countries. But this would be superfluous. The politics of personal rule clearly erode bureaucratic norms and practices, thereby introducing massive waste and indiscipline into the public sector. Governmental incapacity to fulfil the role of modern capitalist (or, for that matter, socialist) state stunts development.

How do the activities of transnational corporations fit into this picture? These corporations are of central importance to the health of the capitalist economy; indeed, before independence, the modern sector was largely a foreign enclave. Although this is much less the case now, foreign investment remains a crucial element.

The African state has a delicate task – to attract *and* regulate transnational corporations. On the one hand, governments should promote foreign investment, because a number of industries will benefit from the technology, technical expertise and international marketing that transnationals can offer. On the other hand, governments should control these corporations because the latter's goal is to maximize profits on a *global* basis and this imperative will conflict with certain local economic priorities. The postwar technological revolution in communications, transport and the processing of information has allowed international firms to centralize their world-wide operations. Head-quarters in New York, London, Paris or Tokyo makes new investments, allocates export markets and research development programmes among its branches in various countries, chooses technology and determines prices charged on intra-firm transactions. These firms have many opportunities, therefore, to advance their own interests at the expense of host countries.

It is, for example, normal business practice for a corporation to minimize its total tax obligation and circumvent the exchange control regulations that govern many countries. Transfer pricing is one means through which these goals are achieved. This involves the manipulation of prices charged on exchanges between a firm's branches located in different jurisdictions in order to transfer profits to companies in countries with lower corporate taxes and minimal or non-existent exchange controls. If a Canadian branch of a corporation sells its second-hand machinery to an associated Kenyan enterprise, for instance, the price will be set not by the market, but by the global profit considerations of the pertinent transnational. In addition, head offices can charge its branches royalties on any technology or trademarks transferred to them, fees for managerial services, interest on loans and a share of its total research and development budget. The discretionary setting of these charges will reflect a corporation's concern to show profits in certain countries but not in others.

Governments should attempt to counter this logic of global profitability in order to maximize local accumulation and growth. They should want to expand their fiscal base by taxing corporate profits. They should seek to augment their foreign exchange holdings by pressing transnationals to expand exports and decrease imports. They may try to persuade foreign firms to expand employment by using less capital-intensive production techniques than those favoured by headquarters. They should attempt to erode the foreigners' monopoly of technical expertise by requiring some local research and development to train indigenous employees. In these ways, the state can protect local interests.

Even the most competent and honest government runs into trouble when it comes to negotiating a favourable contract with foreign firms. Transnationals have considerable bargaining power in certain fields – mineral extraction and processing, agribusiness and manufacturing – because they control research-intensive and sophisticated process and product technologies and international marketing channels. The result is predictable; countries compete for the limited foreign investment. They lure these firms with such incentives as tax holidays, exemptions on import duties, state controls on labour unions and the prohibition of strikes.

However, the politics of personal rule can undermine these efforts to attract and monitor foreign investors. On the one hand, an uncertain political climate discourages foreign firms from committing their capital. On the other hand, malaise, administrative corruption and utter incompetence permit corporations to evade an African state's regulatory efforts. State decay, therefore, has a negative impact in economic terms; it limits both the local stock of direct foreign investment and the local benefits from that which ventures into this insecure environment.

Several factors influence the flow of direct foreign investment. Transnational corporations will not, of course, show any interest in countries whose raw economic potential is low. Mining companies must sink their capital wherever large and accessible reserves of oil or scarce minerals are located. Although these firms would prefer to exploit mineral deposits in politically secure countries like Australia and Canada, the exigencies of global competition compel investment in such resource-rich countries as Nigeria and Ghana – despite their instability. Mines, in any case, can insulate themselves from some of the political turmoil by carving out protected enclaves in their isolated areas. And the same holds true for plantation agriculture. But investments in manufacturing and services are more sensitive to political and administrative conditions. Those countries without large domestic markets for manufactures must construct an exceptional investment climate to entice manufacturing transnationals. Such small countries as the Ivory Coast and Kenya built such an environment in the 1960s and 1970s, and reaped the benefits.

'Investment codes' are promulgated by many governments to create an attractive investment climate. Their aim is simple: attract foreign capital, technology and expertise into particular industries by offering a variety of guarantees and concessions. Typically, these codes provide a guarantee against nationalization without fair compensation. They also specify favourable rules governing the mobility of capital, the transfer of profits, royalties and interest and the concessions on import duties that investors will enjoy. On paper, the codes are impressive. But transnational corporations will still want assurance that these promises, along with specific concessions negotiated with the host government, will be honoured by a prospective challenger to political power. Flagrant violations of the law such as Amin's expropriation of Asian assets following his Ugandan *coup* cloud the future for all investors.

As a consequence of all these factors, foreign investment in Africa is minimal. In 1972, the entire continent accounted for only one-fifth of the total stock of direct foreign investment in the world's developing countries – and of this fifth, the bulk was located in South Africa and North Africa. The core of Africa's investment, almost 62 per cent, was in petroleum, mining and smelting; only 18 per cent involved manufacturing. In contrast, Latin America with a comparable population could boast just over half of the Third World's total direct foreign investment, and almost 40 per cent of this fell into the crucial manufacturing sector. Today, Africa has even less of global foreign investment.

In subsaharan Africa, the major concentrations of foreign capital are in Nigeria, Zaire, Gabon, Liberia, Kenya and the Ivory Coast. Other significant recipients include Zimbabwe, Zambia, Senegal, Ghana and Cameroon. And starting from a small base, foreign investment grew rapidly in Botswana, Gambia and Somalia in the sixties and seventies. Negligible foreign capital has flowed to a number of countries, mainly landlocked ones with small populations and no significant mineral resources such as Burundi, Chad, Equatorial Guinea, Lesotho, Mali, Rwanda and Upper Volta.[18]

Not only is foreign investment often limited, but governments have not effectively regulated those foreign firms that do establish themselves. Two major impediments thwart regulation. First, African countries are extremely dependent upon the West, both economically and politically. A handful of countries – France, Britain and the United States in particular – account for most foreign trade, external loans, foreign investment and aid from abroad. These powers also act as external protectors of many friendly regimes. This dependence ensures that Western nations, their corporations and the IMF, the West's financial disciplinarian, hold considerable influence with African rulers. Since 1977 and the worsening economic situation, this dependency has grown more marked. As transnationals bargain for exemptions and concessions, they discover an even more favourable position.

State decay is the second impediment. Bluntly put, the capacity to control foreign capital is often just not there.

Part of the problem is simply *a lack of will*. Many influential nationals, as we shall see, are happy to collude with foreign corporations which evade regulations aimed at augmenting national control and maximizing national priorities. The philosophy of some entrepreneurs vis-à-vis the foreigners is something like the old adage: if you can't beat them (that is, compete with them), join them. The other aspect is the indiscipline and incompetence of neopatrimonial regimes. Because some bureaucrats are inept or dishonest, transnationals can circumvent the law. Hence, the proclamation of a panoply of rules governing foreign investment does not mean that international firms will contribute more to capitalist development – that they will expand employment opportunities, improve their export performance, accelerate the transfer of skills and expertise or augment local capital formation.

African regimes have followed one or more of three strategies vis-à-vis transnationals. First, they have announced a host of rules controlling economic transnationals. Second, they have instituted indigenization laws to exclude foreign capital from certain sectors and compel local participation in large undertakings. And third, some foreign assets have been wholly or partly nationalized, vesting control in joint (public–private) ventures or wholly public corporations. Rarely do these programmes work out as intended.

There are many ironies at work. For example, regulations designed to improve public scrutiny of corporate activities often simply promote corruption. Firms must typically obtain various licences, permits and certificates before engaging in various economic acts. Inevitably, these controls create bottlenecks which, in turn, invite corrupt dealings; indeed, this may have been the initial intention. In such countries as Nigeria, informal procedures for dealing with the bureaucracy are widely recognized. As a matter of course, foreign corporations employ local middlemen, or facilitators, to intercede with public officials to obtain favourable decisions – for a price.[19] The net result of regulation may be further entrenchment of systemic corruption.

Indigenization laws aim to promote local enterprise and enhance national economic control. Countries that have instituted this sort of programme include Nigeria, Zaire, Ghana, Kenya, Zambia, Uganda and Malawi. Their goals are rarely achieved. Such legislation has raised investors' uncertainty about a government's commitment to safeguarding foreign property rights without actually increasing local control of foreign corporations. Although indigenization has extended the assets of local businessmen, this has been achieved at a high cost. Indigenization does not foster entrepreneurial risk-taking behaviour, which is the essence of capitalist dynamism. Instead, it encourages political insiders to grow wealthy by manipulating political position. Inevitably, political insiders and their partners are the principal beneficiaries of indigenization, for they are the ones to whom transnationals turn for political protection, and they are the ones with access to credit with which to purchase equity.

Zaire provides an extreme case of the failure of indigenization.[20] The imperatives of personal rule, not economic nationalism *per se*, motivated Zairianization. Mobutu envisaged this as a strategy to consolidate his power by distributing lucrative businesses to his followers. Economic nationalism functioned as the ideological pretext for further enrichment of his coterie in the governing party, state apparatus and army. Mobutu confiscated, on 30 November 1973, small and medium wholesale and retail businesses, factories, farms and plantations owned by foreigners. One year later, he took another step as part of his so-called *radicalisation* measures; he expropriated somewhat larger foreign businesses. According to a very simple formula, the government transferred these assets to Zairois *acquéreurs* (acquirers) – the higher one's political position in the political or administrative hierarchy, the grander one's acquisitions. Approximately 2,000 Zairois became instant property-owners in 1973 alone.

But things went badly and within a year of *radicalisation* Mobutu had to retreat. Zairianization brought extensive economic dislocation as inexperienced *acquéreurs* bankrupted their new enterprises almost as speedily as they had acquired them. As well, the President was on the defensive because of a slide in the world price of copper, Zaire's major export. Therefore, 1976 became the year of *retrocession*, that is a return of the expropriated property to its former owners, most of whom were able to reclaim their businesses by mid 1977. This chaotic episode further reduced investors' confidence in the Zairian government and nudged the modern sector yet closer to collapse.

Elsewhere, indigenization has not been this catastrophic. President Amin's expropriation of Asian assets had a comparable economic effect. However, in other countries economic damage was minimized by the ability of foreigners to circumvent regulations and retain control of their assets.

Consider Nigeria, a country with very stringent indigenization laws. The Nigerian Enterprises Promotion Decrees of 1972 and 1977 tried to restrict foreign capital to technologically complex, large-scale operations. By 1977, even the largest foreign firms were obliged to sell either 40 or 60 per cent of their equity (depending on the firm's category) to Nigerians. By 1980, a total of 1,858 had complied with this legislation, selling 500 million shares worth more than $US 800 million to local businessmen.[21]

But transnationals discovered ways to retain control of their enterprises.[22] First, they employed a variety of legal strategies to this end. For instance, if a company had to divest itself of 60 per cent of its equity, it ensured that no other single shareholder held a significant block of shares. Or the firm changed its voting rules to require a two-thirds or three-quarters majority to alter established procedures at board or general meetings. If a firm entered into a joint venture with one or two Nigerian partners, one aspect of the arrangement might be a 'technical services agreement', leaving control over technology choice to the foreign partner. A more complex strategy was to divide diversified manufacturing firms into two: a manufacturing company that would be required to sell only 40 per cent of its equity, and a distribution firm that would have to undertake a 60 per cent divestment. The new manufacturing firm thereby remained firmly under foreign control and this firm could ensure virtual control of its distributing arm as well.

Some corporations also responded to the legislation in more unethical or illegal ways. One strategy was to recruit a nominal local partner who contributed little capital or effort but offered political protection. Another response was to ignore certain provisions – for instance, the requirement to divest by a certain proportion – in the hope of avoiding detection for as long as possible. Finally, some companies were not above resorting to bribery to obtain 'exemptions' from the law. Nigerian managers were simply instructed to 'get the job done'.

National control or local accumulation, it seems, are rarely much advanced by indigenization. As well, the policy frightens foreign investors, feeds corruption and diverts local capital into foreign-controlled enterprises. The following assessment of the Nigerian programme has a wider applicability:

Indigenisation makes more possible the purchase of shares from transnational corporations, enterprises with the best reputation for a safe, profitable return. [. . .] There are no counterincentives for investments in indigenously controlled enterprises, hence the program undermines the basis of accumulation by a national, capitalist class. [...] Indigenisation thus encourages a comprador role for local business in a society already plagued by strong comprador tendencies.[23]

Nationalization is a final means by which some regimes try to maximize local control and benefits from foreign investments. All or part of a particular firm's equity is expropriated, usually with compensation. A wave of nationalizations hit Africa in the 1960s and 1970s. According to a United Nations Survey, there were more expropriations in Africa than any other region in the period 1960–74, 39 per cent of the 875 recorded instances. Takeovers were common even in countries with a capitalist orientation. Of those countries with an attractive target, only the Ivory Coast, Gabon and Liberia desisted. Certain extremely poor countries were not tempted to follow suit; without major foreign investments, Gambia, Central African Republic, Chad, Rwanda and Malawi watched from the sidelines.

The most common targets for expropriation have been public utilities, local branches of international banks and insurance companies, firms engaged in the export trade and mining and petroleum companies. Manufacturing concerns and agribusinesses are the least vulnerable to nationalization, largely because of their dependence on foreign inputs, technology, and in the case of agribusiness, foreign markets.[24]

Our earlier discussion of parastatals indicates the sort of problems that nationalization creates in neopatrimonial systems. With expropriation, the spoils system expands into public utilities, banks and productive enterprises. This curtails economic growth in one or more of three ways: scarce finance capital is illegally siphoned off into the unproductive private enterprises of the ruling elite; foreign suppliers are allowed to make unconscionable profits through deals involving kickbacks; and politically appointed executives who are generally inexperienced or incompetent reduce the productivity of the capital invested in parastatals. The depredations of equipment suppliers in Africa are legendary. In many countries, the ministers in charge of parastatals are popularly known as 'Mr. Ten Percent'.[25]

How can these difficulties be avoided? Some regimes attempt to minimize managerial problems through joint ventures with transnational corporations. Others hire expatriate management teams to operate publicly-owned corporations. But these solutions spawn new problems. If the intention of nationalization was to augment local control and benefits, foreign managers will not serve this purpose. After all, their primary loyalty lies with their parent companies. This can produce conflicts of interest manifest, for instance, in decisions concerning the purchase of machinery and supplies, transfer pricing policy and export marketing policy. Commonly, a public corporation loses money year after year while the foreign corporation involved reaps high rewards.[26]

In sum, capitalism cannot thrive in the context of personal rule and state decay. Although opportunities for profit still exist, these mainly involve the manipulation of the state rather than risk-taking entrepreneurial activity. For example, large firms will invest only if they can exploit a state-supported monopoly position or an accessible and valued natural resource. The manufacturing sector is usually dominated by the branches of transnational corporations or joint ventures involving the latter. As transnationals demand tariff protection and other privileges before sinking capital into manufacturing enterprises, branch plants or joint ventures have no incentive to raise their productivity; they simply pass higher costs on to the consumer. Neither is there any incentive to push exports as their products are not competitive outside protected markets. And because the exchange rate is generally over-valued, the beneficial impact of manufacturing firms is further lessened. If they can obtain it, foreign capital is cheap. This encourages firms to import equipment and intermediate products and discourages them from developing local linkages to ancillary industries. This is not the basis for dynamic capitalist development.

In the resource sector, joint ventures can continue to operate profitably when world prices are high. But the ruling elite must establish protected and well-serviced enclaves. In Zaire, for example, cooperation among the government, transnational mining corporations and foreign governments (French, Belgian, American) allows the functioning of export-oriented mineral enclaves despite economic collapse and political disorder. The state maintains the needed services and security in the enclaves, while foreign governments provide aid and troops to reimpose order when Mobutu's army loses control. Outside these enclaves, economic life languishes; services deteriorate, peasants retreat to subsistence agriculture, and the parallel or black market thrives. Happily, the situation elsewhere is generally not so horrendous. But Zaire must stand as a warning of the economic crisis which state decay can engender.

Political insiders monopolize a third opportunity for profit. Lush state contracts, monopolies in trade and transport, and graft channel scarce resources into a few hands. In principle, this process could promote primitive accumulation by indigenous entrepreneurs. Graft, after all, can fuel capitalism just as well as the self-denying savings of the puritan. But in practice, a good share of the spoils of office are wasted on such things as conspicuous consumption, real estate speculation and foreign holdings. The considerable number of Mercedes-Benz and other luxury vehicles in most African cities attest to the elite's opulent lifestyle. When

officials earning $300–400 per month purchase cars worth
$US 15,000–20,000, something is amiss. In East Africa the
wealthy class is popularly called *wabenzi* – for good reason.
Foreign bank deposits and investments are also popular
with the wealthy leaders. Even Houphouët-Boigny has
publicly admitted stashing billions of francs CFA in Swit-
zerland on the grounds that 'any intelligent politician does
so'.[27] The elite's propensity for export of earnings and
unproductive speculation are reported by commissions of
inquiry in several countries.[28]

Sultanism, or the decay of patrimonial states, does not,
therefore, close off all opportunities for making profits.
Some continue: however, these do not sustain healthy economic growth. Opportunities for easy rewards through
political manipulation divert entrepreneurial efforts into
largely unproductive economic activities. The modern capitalist economy stagnates, helped along by a hostile international economic climate.

The downward spiral of state decay and economic decline create a parasitical ruling elite, widespread shortages
and shrinking real incomes. Desperate people turn to clandestine economic transactions to make ends meet. These are
the transactions of the parallel or informal economy, those
which generate incomes and assets that largely escape enu-
meration and taxation and operate in contravention of
government regulations. For many individuals, these activities represent a survival mechanism. Nonetheless, the expansion of a parallel economy accelerates the downward
spiral to the ultimate detriment of the majority.

Magendo in East Africa, *kalabule* in Ghana – the parallel
economy has various labels. But the activities to which the
name refers are remarkably similar from country to
country. One is the hoarding and exchange of goods above
the official or justified market price. The more scarce a

particular commodity, the more the black market thrives. With a constant demand meeting a reduced supply, the stage is set for middlemen to corner the market and gouge the consumer. Smuggling is another prominent activity: precious metals, lucrative cash crops, archaeological treasures and manufactured goods are the most popular items. And illegal foreign currency deals are also significant in countries with overvalued exchange rates and/or exchange controls. Businessmen who feel threatened find a way to liquidate their assets and export their funds to a safe country, regardless of local currency regulations.

Certain illegal practices are also essential to the operation of the parallel economy. One of these is bribery and corruption. The black market could not exist without the collusion of public officials. Bribes are forthcoming to those who issue import licences and foreign exchange permits, administer price controls, enforce customs regulations and investigate corrupt practices. Also intimately linked with *magendo* is tax evasion. Bribes and illegal commissions are certainly not reported as taxable income. And most money made in the black market is unrecorded and, thus, untaxed. Clearly, the government loses considerable revenue in this manner. The larger the parallel economy, the weaker the fiscal basis of the state.

Failure to arrest the downward spiral will mean an increasingly complex, organized and widespread informal economy. In extreme cases such as Uganda in 1980, *magendo* will equal in value two-thirds or more of the monetary Gross Domestic Product.[29] As the population is drawn into its activities, almost everyone becomes a speculator and, technically, a lawbreaker. But participants have a different perspective. They regard themselves as carrying on commerce despite the obstructions of a parasitical state apparatus. They feel their evasions of regulations are necessary because officials instituted these only to enrich themselves through bribes.

Consider some particular examples of the parallel economy. In West Africa, smuggling and illegal currency deals are
rampant. In Ghana and Nigeria, for instance, exchange
controls and overvalued currencies feed a brisk black-
market trade in currencies. In neighbouring francophone
countries, the Ghanaian cedi (until 1984) and Nigerian naira
exchange for francs CFA at an unofficial rate several times
the official one.

A vast and intricate clandestine trade in commodities also
links the countries of this region. Nigeria's chief smuggling
partners are Benin and Niger, while Ghana trades illegally
with Togo, the Ivory Coast and Burkina Fasso, and Gambia
with Senegal. So extensive is current smuggling that it has
transformed border crossings into booming towns and
markets. Formerly depressed zones in Benin and Niger
bordering on Nigeria and on Togo's border with Ghana are
now among the most prosperous in their countries.[30]

This illegal trade falls into a pattern. In the south–north
trade, Nigerian and Ghanaian participants supply mainly
manufactured goods. In exchange, smugglers in Niger and
Burkina Fasso furnish domestic animals, skins and dried
lake-fish. The east–west trade between anglophone and
francophone countries is more complex. Smuggling in both
directions involves a mix of manufactured and agricultural
products. Cocoa and most other cash crops are smuggled
from the three anglophone countries to their francophone
neighbours. Peanuts are the exception; they flow out of
Senegal and Niger to satisfy the high demand in Gambia and
Nigeria.

A couple of cases in point will illustrate the extent of this
illegal trade.[31] In 1981, the value of smuggled goods between
Nigeria and Benin was an estimated 12 billion francs
CFA ($US 58 million). Seeking to evade import controls,
Nigerian businessmen used Benin's port of Cotonou as their
major conduit of illegal overseas imports. Jewels, liquor,
cigarettes, tobacco and lace are the major items in this re-

export trade. In return, Nigerians supplied Benin with smuggled detergents, household appliances, electronics, cars and car parts and motor fuel. In fact, fuel represented about half of the value of Benin's fraudulent imports.

The deterioration of Ghana's formal economy and the imposition of import controls encouraged a thriving illegal trade with all its neighbours. This trade, between Ghana and Togo for example, totalled 5.7 billion francs CFA ($US 27.5 million) in 1981, according to the Central Bank of West African States. From the Togolese, Ghanaians got such banned imports as tobacco, cigarettes, alcohol and fine Dutch textiles as well as a range of other scarce commodities. Ghanaians, for their part, smuggled cocoa, vegetables, fruit, eggs, diamonds, kitchen utensils and metal beds and mattresses into Togo.

Cocoa is of major significance. Because the Ghanaian marketing board until 1983 paid him a low price (owing to the overvaluation of the cedi) following a long delay, the grower preferred the more lucrative returns if his crop was smuggled into Togo or the Ivory Coast. He also received his money immediately and could convert his francs CFA into cedis on the black market at an advantageous rate. A 30Kg headload of cocoa that sold for 360 cedis in Ghana in 1981 could fetch the equivalent of 1,300–1,400 cedis in Togo. Even with the expenses of transport and bribes, the grower was much better off. It is not surprising, therefore, that in 1980 an estimated 80 per cent of the cocoa grown in the Volta Region was simply left unharvested or smuggled across the nearby Togo border.[32]

The strictly internal dimensions of the parallel economy also deserve a few words. Ghana is a striking example of the decline of the formal economy and the expansion of the black market. Widespread smuggling and illegal currency dealings were accompanied by the hoarding and sale of goods at inflated prices. Before Ft.-Lieutenant Rawlings imposed draconian measures in 1983, black marketeers hoarded and exchanged both foodstuffs and goods smuggled from neighbouring countries. Even food aid found its way onto the black market. The politicians blamed the market women for hoarding, but they were only part of a chain.

In fact, the market women, like others, were trying to defend their living standards by dealing in *kalabule*. In the 1970s, *kalabule* became an increasingly complex and organized marketing system. Large organizations emerged which both transported agricultural products from rural areas to avoid marketing boards, and marketed the commodities at the prevailing black market prices to escape price controls. The government's simple expedient of harassing market women and closing down markets could not eradicate the black market. It did, however, make the public's daily task of locating supplies even more trying.

A similar pattern of smuggling, illegal currency transactions and hoarding exists in Eastern and Central Africa. One network of illegal trade involves Kenya, the Southern Sudan, Uganda and Zaire, with minor involvement of Tanzania and others.[33] The case of Uganda deserves special mention as its parallel economy overshadows the formal economy.

Uganda manifests the same symptoms of economic and political decay and a burgeoning black market as Ghana. Before 1972, the Ugandan economy was one of the most prosperous in Eastern Africa. Roads, schools, hospitals and other services were, in general, excellent, as was the administrative system. But Amin's regime swiftly wrecked the formal economy, beginning with his expulsion of the Asians in 1972. A rapacious ruling elite and economic decline drove more and more people into *magendo* activities. As elsewhere, Uganda's *magendo* sprang from a scarce supply of most commodities. In 1981, one observer reported:

Normal shops were virtually non-existent. Those which appear to operate are limited to 'selected' clienteles or are almost wholly unstocked. Postage stamps, electricity, telephone calls, telegraph services, airplane tickets and (less certainly) the government newspaper are usually moderately available at fixed, 'legal' prices in Kampala – but nothing else.[34]

The result is a complex, highly organized parallel economy. 'Families' resembling organized crime syndicates arrange the transport, the illegal trade, the bribes and the finance that facilitate *magendo*. Troublemakers are neatly dealt with by their 'security' forces. The inadequacy of salaries and wages in relation to prevailing prices binds the majority to black market activities. There is a saying in Kampala which has more than a ring of truth – 'to eat *magendo* one must earn *magendo*'.

The cases of Zaire, Ghana and Uganda graphically illustrate the perils of the downward spiral. As the formal economy and state capacity deteriorate, people scramble for ways to deal with falling living standards and shortages. The result is the parallel economy. Yet the expansion of this accelerates economic and political decay. As the black market is a parasite feeding upon resources from the formal economy and undercutting prices by means of smuggling and tax evasion, economic problems worsen. Political life also fares poorly. State decay is a necessary condition for the emergence of *kalabule* and *magendo*. The parallel economy cannot thrive without the evasion of regulations and taxes by the bribing of officials. However, the black market contributes, in turn, to the debility of the government; it not only deepens systemic corruption, but also shrinks the state's fiscal basis.

Economic decline, state decay and the extension of the black market are, thus, mutually reinforcing. Can this downward spiral be reversed? It is a difficult task to be sure, not least because the people who should reform the system – the politicians and bureaucrats – stand to lose the most.

§ 7 §

SURVIVAL STRATEGIES

'Pessimism of the intellect, optimism of the will' – this Gramscian dictum points a balanced approach to the African crisis. 'Pessimism of the intellect' is unavoidable in light of the grim situation facing many countries. Independence brought neither democracy nor prosperity to most Africans. Self-rule there was, but often with a pronounced economic and military dependence on external powers. The economic aspects of this crisis we have traced to a variety of factors, both endogenous and exogenous. Intractable realities of geography, demography and climate dictate a meagre economic potential for some. A harsh international economic environment assails all of Africa, and accelerates the downward spiral. And socio-political conditions hamper a capitalist breakthrough. Africa's peasant societies, with their poorly adapted institutions, weakly integrated communities and minimal class formation, have not evolved into effective capitalist states. Their neopatrimonial regimes operate in ways discordant with the requirements for capital accumulation and capitalist growth.

What, then, are the grounds for 'optimism of the will'? Given the constraints illustrated in this book, is it not merely foolish to hold out fond hopes for Africa's future? No – we must believe that people make history despite objective constraints. We can anticipate that Africans, refusing to be the helpless victims of overpowering forces, will find a creative response to their predicament.

But where is the road forward? How can the downward spiral be checked and reversed? We hesitate to offer advice, for Africa is already awash with foreigners proferring counsel. We will provide instead only some reflections upon the feasibility of certain remedies and strategies from the perspective which our analysis suggests.

One thing is sure. Africa cannot sit passively by and wait for a reformed world economy to solve its problems. A New International Economic Order (NIEO), demanded by Third World governments and reform-minded intellectuals since the early 1970s, will not arrive. This demand stems from the reasonable view that the present international order operates inequitably. Spokesmen have issued a number of proposals: greater access of the South to developed countries' markets, especially for manufactured goods; more stable and higher prices for the primary commodity exports of the South; controls to prevent abuses associated with the transfer of capital and technology by transnational corporations; the right to nationalize firms exploiting natural resources; and greater availability of credit from reformed international monetary and development agencies (especially the IMF and World Bank).

In 1980, the well-known first report of the Brandt Commission (the Report of the Independent Commission on International Development Issues) entitled *North–South: A Programme for Survival* endorsed many of these proposals. It argued that a restructured and reformed international economic and political order would benefit *all* the world's people. 'International solidarity', the report observes, 'must stem from strong mutual interest in cooperation and from compassion for the hungry.'

Stirring words do not, however, always produce the desired results. Western governments were not prodded into a conciliatory mood. A decade of negotiations amply attests to these governments' hesitancy to accept any reform of the international order that penalizes their economies in the short run. The problem is that the 'harmony of interests' preached by Brandt functions only in the long term. If the South enjoyed renewed prosperity, the demand for the sophisticated manufactured products of industrial countries would indeed eventually swell. But the short term is what concerns governments in these industrial countries, especially in the context of a recession. While unemployment and inflation plague their citizens, politicians reject changes which necessitate expensive adjustments at home. In any event, alterations of the international economic order have never been effected because of social injustice and long-term mutual interest. They rather become *faits accomplis* as a consequence of a shifting international power balance. Because the North remains economically strong, the NIEO is unlikely to be born soon.

In fact, low-income developing countries in Africa would derive relatively few benefits from NIEO in any case. The Newly Industrializing Countries (NICs), being able to expand their manufactured exports and attract loans from the World Bank and private banks, would accrue the most advantages. But there are no NICs in subsaharan Africa. This region would probably benefit only from the proposed stabilization and raising of raw material prices and from higher aid. Indeed, foreign aid will continue to be an important item in Africa's balance of payments. For this reason, the World Bank has called for a doubling of concessional assistance to tropical Africa between 1980 and 1990.[1]

Finally, which members of African societies would actually benefit from an increased inflow of resources stemming from international reform? Given the current national power structures, foreign earnings might simply finance the import of more luxury goods and weapons. Such a pattern would have two negative results: the repressive potential of African states would be reinforced as would the stake of the ruling elite in an inequitable social order. Broadly based prosperity and democracy are not part of this picture.

Africans must look to domestic responses to their crisis. The realities of the international economy and the immensity of the problems confronting the people compel this conclusion. Of course, the international order *does* need reform. But we must recognize Africa's limited economic power – and thus its limited capacity to force or benefit from a new international order.

And what might these responses be? We can identify three for further examination.

1. *Avoid the state.* In the context of economic deterioration and a corrupt and incapacitated state, local self-reliance is the prime survival strategy for the majority. Local communities in Zaire, Chad, Ghana, Uganda and the Sudan cannot expect to build a better life through assistance from central authorities and planning agencies. They must fend for themselves. Usually, this will entail efforts to improve their informal economies so that many of their basic needs can be satisfied locally or through trade with nearby communities.

This is how Ghanaians have coped with the collapse of their formal economy. In the 1970s, urban employees tried to compensate for the declining purchasing power of their salaries with trading activities, farming, the raising of cattle, and poultry production. As the decade wore on, a growing number of people withdrew from employment altogether. Tens of thousands of professionals, skilled and unskilled employees emigrated to more prosperous African countries or abroad. But others, for family or other reasons, decided to stay. Some of these urbanites retreated from the towns, driven out by violent crime as well as deteriorating services and escalating *kalabule* prices, to their natal countryside communities. Among those returning were highly trained professionals such as medical doctors, midwives, dentists, architects and engineers.

This population movement gave impetus to village economies. Communities had to provide their own services and much of their own food and manufactures. In many southern villages, the emphasis shifted from export crops (especially cocoa) to foodstuffs. Farmers marketed their produce through their own channels, disregarding political boundaries, marketing boards and official prices. Villagers substituted local products for commodities formerly purchased from stores. Shea butter-nut oil replaced cooking oil. Locally crafted ceramic cooking utensils replaced factory-made metal ones. As tools were also now unavailable from the towns, people substituted local cutlasses. There was a return to the practice of building one's own house with local materials. All this required the resuscitation of crafts that had fallen into disuse – those of the potter, the tinker and the blacksmith. A territory-wide extension of these activities meant an expansion of the parallel economy, to the point that the term became wholly misleading.[2]

Other countries facing the same economic and political situation have witnessed the same recrudescence of local self-reliance and self-sufficiency. In the peripheral communities of southern Sudan or Tanzania, for instance, this survival strategy was perhaps less painful than in southern Ghana since communities were less involved in national markets. Those with one foot still in subsistence production are less troubled by the necessity to resort to local self-sufficiency. Although villagers missed commodities such as kerosene or paraffin and sugar, ingenious people found substitutes. In the Bukoba Region of Tanzania, for instance, villagers who could not buy paraffin bought used tires to burn rubber for illumination. When the local *duka* (store) no longer stocked sugar, they resumed a more traditional diet, for example, *ugali* for breakfast sweetened with banana juice which had been popular before the 1960s. This porridge was inexpensive and nutritious.[3]

This recourse to self-reliance is certainly a creative adaptation to a deteriorating situation. Many communities have, by insulating themselves from the formal economy and the state, lessened the decline of their living standards. And in so doing, the people have unwittingly demonstrated the practicability of one current school of development theory. Some writers regard this focus on small-scale community solutions as preferable under *any* circumstances. As one self-identified 'barefoot economist' working in Latin America writes: 'I believe in local action and in small dimensions. It is only in such environments that human activity and meaningful identities can truly surface and flourish.'[4]

According to this 'development as liberation' school, grassroots self-reliance can prove liberating in two senses.[5] First, such programmes can free small communities *from* something – the rigours of material deprivation. In addition, participatory development can be liberating in a broader sense. Through defining their own needs, designing and implementing their own projects, villagers educate themselves in organizational dynamics and self-government. In time, this local capacity for organization and confidence may increase popular pressure for change at the territorial level. Or so it is hoped.

Ideally, grassroots development would be the focus of Western aid. Non-governmental organizations (NGOs) are generally better suited to this sort of project than national aid agencies. Strict bureaucratic procedures governing resource transfers, a proclivity for large and capital-intensive projects and an acute desire not to offend the governments of recipient countries – all this constrains the latter's effectiveness at the grassroots. NGOs such as Oxfam, Development and Peace, Voluntary Service Overseas, Canadian University Students Overseas are not overwhelmed by the same constraints. In addition, they usually employ dedicated people who respect local cultures and hold a positive philosophy of development. This conceives of foreign aid as most useful when it helps communities to help themselves by developing self-reliance, autonomy and productivity at the local level.[6] In contemporary Africa, this orientation will likely prove the most beneficial.

But we must not let romantic notions carry us away. The fact is that local self-reliance, though a creative response, is nonetheless a coping or survival strategy. It is not really a long-term substitute for the creation of a healthy national economy with orderly, responsive political institutions at the centre. Further, if the formation of national identities and national classes are prerequisites for national reconstruction, then village self-reliance obstructs such social changes. For the buttressing of local communities is likely to consolidate communal not class or national identities and action. Thus, the implications of this coping mechanism are not wholly positive.

2. *Free the markets*. Others, mainly economists, propose a different response – release market forces by trimming the bureaucracy, reducing administrative bottlenecks and relying more upon private entrepreneurs. This option is obviously compatible with the survival strategy just discussed. Any practical reform programme must recognize the prevalence of local self-reliance and unregulated economic activity. A logical strategy at the centre, therefore, is to conceive of the state's role as complementing these innovative adaptations. The government must allow the economy to operate more freely; that is, it must come to terms with reality, and accordingly, shrink its regulatory and participatory roles. Some argue that it should focus solely on the reconstruction of roads, ports, railways, telephone

systems, schools, hospitals and sanitation, the fixing of higher producer prices for agricultural exports and the re-establishment of law and order. This is a modest but, under the circumstances, perhaps more suitable role.

The 'Agenda for Action' proposed by the World Bank in 1981 fits this orientation. Its report, *Accelerated Development in Sub-Saharan Africa*, identifies four major factors underlying Africa's economic woes: the neglect of smallholder agriculture; the bias toward import-substituting manufacturing industries, manifest particularly in high tariff protection; the overvaluation of African currencies which again favours manufacturing over agriculture; and the overly extensive and inefficient state economic intervention. A myriad of specific proposals are outlined to deal with each of these shortcomings. The overall strategy is to increase production, especially of agricultural and mineral exports, by offering greater opportunities to private initiative. This will require the state to utilize more efficiently its resources, stop providing certain expensive services and allow market forces more freedom in determining prices.

Although the report identifies some real flaws in policy and administration, its apolitical and ahistorical orientation seriously limits its usefulness as a guide to action. The report is ahistorical in that it does not recognize the central role played everywhere by governments in capitalist development since the Great Depression. There is nothing unusual about the weight of the public sector in subsaharan African countries.[7] When their public expenditure as a proportion of gross domestic product is compared to that of developing countries (including NICs) elsewhere, one finds no significant difference. Typically, public spending accounts for about one-quarter of the GDP. Even the distribution of expenditures among the various budgetary items is similar. And in the Western welfare states, government expenditure is proportionately almost twice that typical in Africa. In all parts of the world the story is the same; the state is intimately involved in capitalist economies.

The apolitical approach is also a problem. Although one might expect this of a World Bank document, the same shortcoming mars most neoclassical economic analyses advocating the release of market forces. These generally recommend that governments increase prices to agricultural producers, reduce tariff barriers, realign exchange rates to reflect market values and rationalize and shrink the parastatal sector. But these proposals, in assuming that an economic rationality prevails, misrepresent the mainsprings of state behaviour. Our analysis has shown that the political and economic exigencies of personal rule subvert a capitalist logic. Thus, current policy and mismanagement actually have a *raison d'être* within this political system. It is not the size of the public sector or even the extent of its economic intervention that are at fault. It is the logic that shapes the decisions of politicians and administrators.

This obviously poses a major obstacle to reform. Because the changes suggested by the World Bank would undercut the power and/or wealth of political insiders, they resist the proposals. The fundamental problem is a political one – where is the will to free markets and shrink the state?

3. *Build the state.* A third strategy, again not incompatible with the first two, is to build state capacity. People withdraw from the chaos of the formal economy as the government shows itself totally incapable of effective management. One response is to recognize the state's incapacity by reducing the role of the public sector to a few core functions. Another is to rehabilitate the governmental organization. Only if the state can rebuild the economic infrastructure, provide security for those who obey and try to uphold the law, collect taxes, realign exchange rates and bring salaries and wages into line with the cost of living, can

the parallel economy be brought under control and the downward spiral reversed. These tasks require extensive changes in the operations of many states.

Our analysis has proposed that there are two main aspects to building state capacity. The first is the construction of coherent, competent and committed administrative and regulatory institutions. Today, both capitalist and socialist development place a heavy burden on bureaucratic organizations. The civil servants in African countries are handed a very demanding job: they are expected not only to implement policies efficiently, but also to formulate most of them, mediate social conflicts, regulate foreign economic relations and run corporations. The quality of the public sector is, therefore, a major determinant of economic success. The second aspect of state capacity is the authorities' ability to garner public consent, or at least assent, to government directives. Without this legitimacy, governments cannot govern effectively.

Consider first the buttressing of bureaucratic institutions, a concern of Western aid agencies and social scientists in the 1950s. 'Development administration' was a fashionable issue in the fifties and sixties; then, the developmental process seemed a lot less problematic than it does today. Development administrations were to act as the spearheads of modernization in traditional societies – by planning, coordinating and regulating national development. The aim was, therefore, to build bureaucracies as professionally competent, honest and even politically neutral tools for change. Western experts were to help with their models of bureaucratic organization, training and technical assistance.

Of course, this vision was too rosy. The main problem is that bureaucracy is as much an outcome of modernization as it is its agent. The paradox is that, according to conventional developmental thinking, Africa must depend for modernization upon an instrument that itself requires modernization. Bureaucracy that actually works is part of a process of increasing secularization, organizational complexity, economic development and literacy. Bureaucracy cannot easily be insulated from the society in which it operates (unless foreigners run it). And those which function in neopatrimonial polities will normally be penetrated by the logic of this governing mode. Again, what appears as mismanagement actually has a rationale.

How can neopatrimonial administration change in a bureaucratic direction? Goran Hyden argues in a controversial book that there are 'no shortcuts to progress', that the appearance of an effective state apparatus committed to capitalist policies must await the emergence of a national bourgeoisie whose class power overshadows the independent power of the state.[8] The logic of this position is clear. Capitalism is facilitated by the rise of a capitalist class able to impose discipline and responsiveness upon governmental organization. But the implications are bleak. An independent national bourgeoisie in the classic Western mould is unlikely to appear soon in tropical Africa. Indeed, change is generally in the direction of highly factionalized neopatrimonial systems, not of class societies and modern-style class struggles.

But perhaps the position that Hyden expresses is overly pessimistic. Historically, there have been shortcuts to progress. Not every successful capitalist experiment was attendant upon the installation in power of a strong and independent bourgeoisie. This was the pattern in Britain in the eighteenth and nineteenth centuries. However, it was not the pattern in nineteenth- and twentieth-century Germany, Japan and Taiwan. There, capitalist industrialization has represented a 'revolution from above' carried through by traditionalist oligarchies who recognized the necessity to modernize or perish. Could not similar revolutions from above occur in Africa?

At first glance, this possibility appears unlikely. Tropical

Africa generally lacks national traditional oligarchies to the same extent as it lacks national bourgeoisies. Neither do African states benefit from the legitimacy and influence stemming from cultural homogeneity, tradition, and a widely perceived national threat, as did the modernizing regimes in Germany, Japan and Taiwan. Nonetheless, we cannot rule out the possibility that nationally minded and modernizing bureaucracies led by far-sighted political leaders will emerge here and there. While anterior to a strong bourgeoisie, such regimes would devise and implement policies designed to facilitate its growth. Was this not the role of Félix Houphouët-Boigny and Jomo Kenyatta? What this role demands is a finely honed realism, including an ability to seize opportunities presented by the operation of the world economy and to shield the administrative apparatus from the corruptive impact of neopatrimonialism.

Such a modernizing leadership would face the challenge of building not only an effective bureaucracy, but public support and enthusiasm as well. A state cannot promote rapid socio-economic change in a context of social indiscipline. It must rely upon some combination of coercion and consent to implement its programme. The temptation for a leader faced with mounting problems and dissident voices is to turn increasingly to repression. To this end, he will find a friendly foreign power willing to transfer weapons and coercive technology and train local personnel in their use. Repression can maintain a modicum of political order, provided that the armed forces can be kept in line. But a sullen and hostile population will not cooperate with the social programme pressed by the bureaucracy.

How then can a regime foster voluntary compliance, perhaps the key element of the strong state? The task is formidable in Uganda, Zaire, Ghana, the Sudan and other countries in which the people quite justifiably regard the state *as the problem, not the solution.* One is tempted at this point to advocate democracy as a means of rebuilding consent where faith in government has vanished. Open debate and an unhampered struggle among contending parties for public support can certainly be the most stable basis for popular consent and strong government. Realistically, though, our analysis does not suggest that democracy has any real prospect in the limiting conditions of contemporary Africa. What is the best feasible alternative? Decent, responsive and largely even-handed personal rule. Although neopatrimonialism is virtually the only workable mode of governance in tropical Africa, Houphouët-Boigny's neopatrimonialism is infinitely preferable to that of an Idi Amin. The point is obviously that there is personal rule and personal rule. And that citizens will be more likely to comply voluntarily with the decisions of strongmen who are willing to listen to their grievances and wishes.

Even these survival strategies – shrinking the public sector and freeing markets, rebuilding or defending administrative capacity, and fostering political support – constitute a formidable agenda. More formidable still is the challenge posed by strategies for satisfying basic human needs, the strategies that excited much debate in the late 1970s and early 1980s. Development, we all sadly recognize, is a far more complex and longer term process than was envisaged just a few years ago.

NOTES

I DISAPPOINTMENTS OF INDEPENDENCE

1 See Naomi Chazan, *An Anatomy of Ghanaian Politics, 1969–1982* (Boulder, Col.: Westview, 1983), 173–8.
2 See M.S. Ahluwalia, 'Income Inequality: Some Dimensions of the Problem', in Hollis Chenery *et al., Redistribution with Growth* (London: Oxford University Press, 1974), 3–37; and A. Bequele and R. Van der Hoeven, 'Poverty and Inequality in Sub-Saharan Africa', *International Labour Review*, CIX, 3 (1980), 381–92.

2 WHY CAPITALISM FAILS

1 A clear statement of the neo-Marxian or dependency view is that of R. Harris, 'The Political Economy of Africa – Underdevelopment or Revolution', in Harris, ed., *The Political Economy of Africa* (New York: Schenkman, 1975), 1–47. An opposite view focusing on internal problems is that of P.T. Bauer, *Equality, the Third World and Economic Delusion* (London: Methuen, 1981), Ch. 4.
2 William A. Hence, *Population, Migration and Urbanization in Africa* (New York: Columbia University Press, 1970), 384–6, 420–1.
3 A.M. Kamarick, 'The Resources of Tropical Africa', *Daedalus*, III, 2 (1982), 149.
4 *Ibid.*, 157–8.
5 See Chris Cook and David Killingray, *African Political Facts Since 1945* (New York: Facts on File, 1983), 221–5.
6 A.L. Mabogunje, 'Manufacturing and the Geography of Development in Tropical Africa', *Economic Geography*, XXXIX (1973), 1–3.
7 On Western Europe, see David S. Landes, *The Unbound Prometheus: Technological Change and Industrial Development in Western*

Europe from 1750 to the Present (Cambridge University Press, 1972), 34–9.

8 G. Myrdal, *The Challenge of World Poverty* (New York: Vintage, 1970), 279.

9 See K. Griffin, 'The International Transmission of Inequality', in his *International Inequality and National Poverty* (London: Macmillan, 1978) 13–41; and P. Streeten, 'Approaches to a New International Economic Order', *World Development*, x, 1 (1982), 1–18.

10 See M. Radetski, 'The Potential for Monopolistic Commodity Pricing by Developing Countries', in G.K. Helleiner, ed., *A World Divided* (Cambridge University Press, 1976), 53–76; R. Bissell, 'African Power in International Resource Organizations', *Journal of Modern African Studies*, XVIII, 1 (1979), 1–14.

11 H.S. Marcussen, 'The Ivory Coast Facing the Economic Crisis', in Jerker Carlsson, ed., *Recession in Africa* (Uppsala: Scandinavian Institute of African Studies, 1983).

12 C. Tilly, 'Reflections on the History of European State-Making', in Charles Tilly, ed., *The Formation of National States in Western Europe* (Princeton University Press, 1975), 72–3.

13 For the classic statement, see K. Polanyi, *The Great Transformation: The Political and Economic Origins of our Time* (Boston: Beacon Press, 1944), especially 149–50. See also B. Supple, 'The State and the Industrial Revolution, 1700–1914', in C. Cipolla, ed., *The Fontana Economic History of Europe*, vol. III (London: Fontana, 1973), 302–15.

14 Supple, 'The State and the Industrial Revolution', 302–3. See also Landes, *The Unbound Prometheus*, 15–34.

15 B. Moore, 'Asian Fascism: Japan', in his *Social Origins of Dictatorship and Democracy* (Boston: Beacon Press, 1965), 93–182.

16 D. Landes, 'Japan and Europe: Contrasts in Industrialization', in W. Lockwood, ed., *The State and Economic Enterprise in Japan* (Princeton University Press, 1965), 93–182.

17 A. Amsden, 'Taiwan's Economic History: A Case of Etatism and a Challenge to the Dependency Theory', *Modern China*, V (1979), 341–79; and G. Ranis, 'Equity with Growth in Taiwan: How Special is the Special Case', *World Development*, VI, 3 (1978), 397–410.

18 R. Lemarchand, 'Quelles indépendances?', *Le mois en Afrique* (Fév.–Mars, 1983), 19–37.

19 R. Shaw, 'The Need to Avoid Crisis Management', *The Weekly Review* (Nairobi) (18 Nov., 1983), 27.

20 See Moore, *Social Origins* for a discussion of the two major paths of capitalist industrialization.

21 cf. S. Huntington, 'Political Development and Political Decay', in his *Political Order in Changing Societies* (New Haven, Conn.: Yale University Press, 1968).

3 COLONIAL ROOTS OF THE CONTEMPORARY CRISIS

1 See Peter Wickens, *An Economic History of Africa* (Cape Town: Oxford University Press, 1981), 220–30.

2 W. Connor, 'Nation Building or Nation Destroying?', *World Politics*, XXIV, 3 (1972), 333–5.

3 A good summary of the facilitating factors is in C. Young, 'Patterns of Social Conflict: State, Class and Ethnicity', *Daedalus*, CXI, 2 (1982), 75–89.

4 See Richard Sandbrook, *The Politics of Basic Needs: Urban Aspects of Assaulting Poverty in Africa* (London: Heinemann, 1982), 42–3.

5 Lewis H. Gann, *Burden of Empire: An Appraisal of Western Colonialism in Africa South of the Sahara* (New York: Praeger, 1967), 389–90.

6 See, e.g., E.A. Brett, *Colonialism and Underdevelopment in East Africa* (London: Heinemann, 1973), 288–310; and S.H. Hymer, 'The Political Economy of the Gold Coast', in G. Ranis, ed., *Government and Economic Development* (New Haven, Conn.: Yale University Press, 1971), 131–68.

7 K. Post, '"Peasantization" and Rural Political Movements in Western Africa', *European Journal of Sociology*, XIII, 2 (1972), 223–54.

8 For an elegant statement of class formation in this sense, see E.P. Thompson, *The Making of the English Working Class* (London: Victor Gollancz, 1964), 9–10.

9 See Bob Fitch and Mary Oppenheimer, *Ghana: The End of an Illusion* (New York: Monthly Review Press, 1967).

10 Roger Genoud, *Nationalism and Economic Development in Ghana* (New York: Praeger, 1969), 49.

11 *Ibid*, 169.

4 CLASS, TRIBE AND POLITICS

1 C. Leys, 'Politics in Kenya: The Development of Peasant Society', *British Journal of Political Science*, I (1971), 324. For confirmation, see Chris Leo, *Land and Class in Kenya* (University of Toronto Press, 1984).

2 E.J. Hobsbawm, 'Class Consciousness in History', in Istvan Meszaros, ed., *Aspects of History and Class Consciousness* (London: RKP, 1971), 9.

3 *Ibid*, 9.

4 See R.C. Fox, W. de Craemer and J.M. Ribeaucaut, 'The Second Independence: A Case Study of the Kwilu Rebellion', *Comparative Studies in Society and History*, VIII (1965), 98–105; and C.E.F. Beer and G. Williams, 'The Politics of the Ibadan Peasantry', in Gavin Williams, ed., *Nigeria: Economy and Society* (London: Rex Collings, 1976), 253.

5 See, e.g., N. Swainson, 'State and Economy in Post-Colonial Kenya', *Canadian Journal of African Studies*, XII, 3 (1978), 357–81; Sayre Schatz, *Nigerian Capitalism* (Los Angeles: University of California Press, 1977), 41–62, 161–3; and J.D. Esseks, 'Government and Indigenous Private Enterprise in Ghana', *Journal of Modern African Studies*, IX, 1 (1971), 11–29.

6 C. Leys, 'African Economic Development in Theory and Practice', *Daedalus*, CXI, 2 (1982), 113.

7 *Ibid*, 113.

8 See, e.g., C. Leys, 'Capital Accumulation, Class Formation, and Dependency – The Significance of the Kenyan Case', *The Socialist Register*, 1978, 241–66.

9 Antonio Gramsci, the oft-quoted Italian Marxist, regarded hegemony as the normal form of control in post-feudal societies. See Walter L. Adamson, *Hegemony and Revolution: Antonio Gramsci's Political and Cultural Theory* (Los Angeles: University of California Press, 1980), 170–3.

10 The term used by Goran Hyden in his *No Shortcuts to Progress: African Development Management in Perspective* (Los Angeles: University of California Press, 1983).

11 Anonymous, *Independent Kenya* (London: Zed Press, 1982), 80.

12 Henrik Marcussen and Jens Torp, *Internationalization of Capital: Prospects for the Third World* (London: Zed Press, 1982), 73.

13 See *ibid*, 96, and Y.–A. Fauré et J.–F. Médard, 'Classe dominante ou classe dirigeante?', and J.–M. Gastellu et S.A. Yapi, 'Un mythe à décomposer: la "bourgeoisie de planteurs"', both in Y.-A. Fauré et J.-F. Médard, *État et bourgeoisie en Côte d'Ivoire* (Paris: Éditions Karthala, 1982).

14 R. Sklar, 'The Nature of Class Domination in Africa', *Journal of Modern African Studies*, XVII, 4 (1979), 537.

15 The information in this section is taken from Richard Sandbrook, *The Politics of Basic Needs: Urban Aspects of Assaulting Poverty in Africa* (London: Heinemann, 1982), Ch. 4.

16 J. Gugler, 'On the Theory of Rural-Urban Migration in Africa', in J.A. Jackson, ed., *Migration* (Cambridge University Press, 1969), 146–7.

17 See Sandbrook, *Politics of Basic Needs*, 208–14.

18 For an elaboration of this theme, see R.H. Bates, 'Modernization, Ethnic Competition, and the Rationality of Politics in Contemporary Africa', in Donald Rothchild and Victor Olorunsola, eds., *The State Versus Ethnic Claims* (Boulder, Col.: Westview Press, 1983), 152–71.

19 D. Brown, 'Who are the Tribalists? Social Pluralism and Political Ideology in Ghana', *African Affairs*, LXXXI (1982), 68–9.

20 P. Lubeck, 'Class Formation at the Periphery: Class Consciousness and Islamic Nationalism among Nigerian Workers', in *Research in the Sociology of Work*, I (Greenwich, Conn.: JAI Press, 1981), 37–70.

5 ANATOMY OF PERSONAL RULE

1 Max Weber, *The Theory of Social and Economic Organization* (New York: The Free Press, 1947), 347–57.

2 *Ibid*, 347, and G. Roth, 'Personal Rulership, Patrimonialism, and Empire Building in the New States', *World Politics*, XX, 2 (1968), 194–206.

3 Anonymous, *Independent Kenya* (London: Zed Press, 1982), 14.

4 D.J. Gould, 'The Administration of Underdevelopment', in Guy Gran, ed., *Zaire: The Political Economy of Underdevelopment* (New York: Praeger, 1979), 87–107.

5 Cf. M. Szeftel, 'Political Graft and the Spoils System in Zambia', *Review of African Political Economy*, 24 (1982), 5.

6 Gould, 'Administration of Underdevelopment', 95–9.

7 Quoted in D. J. Gould, 'Patrons and Clients: The Role of the Military in Zaire Politics', in Isaac Mowoe, ed., *The Performance of Soldiers as Governors* (Washington, D.C.: University Press of America, 1980), 485.

8 *Ibid*, 485.

9 *Time Magazine* (16 January 1984), 28.

10 J. Isnard, 'France's Unhappy Spies', *The Guardian Weekly* (11 November 1979), 12.

11 S. R. Weissman, 'CIA Covert Actions in Zaire and Angola: Patterns and Consequences', *Political Science Quarterly*, XCIV, 2 (1979), 285.

12 Cynthia H. Enloe, *Police, Military and Ethnicity: The Foundation of State Power* (New Brunswick, N.J.: Transaction Books, 1980), 21–2. See also, H. Bienen, 'Public Order and the Military in Africa', in Henry Bienen, ed., *The Military Intervenes* (New York: Praeger, 1968), 45.

13 This account draws heavily on J. E. Adekson, 'Ethnicity, the Military, and Domination: The Case of Obote's Uganda, 1962–71', *Plural Societies*, IX, 1 (1978), 89–95.

14 David Martin, *General Amin* (London: Faber and Faber, 1974), 154–7.

15 *Africa Confidential*, XXIV, 12 (18 June 1983), 5.

16 Statistics from David Volman, *A Continent Besieged: Foreign Military Activities in Africa Since 1975*, Report of the Institute for Policy Studies, Washington, D.C., 1981.

17 The data is drawn from *ibid*, 12–13, and Michael Klare and Cynthia Aronson, *Supplying Repression: US Support for Authoritarian Regimes Abroad* (Washington, D.C.: Institute for Policy Studies, 1981), 104–6.

18 R. Luckham, 'French Militarism in Africa', *Review of African Political Economy*, 24 (1982), 55–84.

19 Weissman, 'CIA Covert Actions', 245. See also, R. Lemarchand, 'The CIA in Africa: How Central? How Intelligent?', *Journal of Modern African Studies*, XIV, 4 (1976), 401–26.

6 THE DOWNWARD SPIRAL

1 This case study draws heavily on J. MacGaffey, 'How to Survive and Become Rich Amidst Devastation: The Second Economy in Zaire', *African Affairs*, LXXXII, 328 (1983) 351–66.

2 For this data, see *ibid*.

3 For the six instances, see V.T. LeVine, 'The Politics of Presidential Succession', *Africa Report*, XXVIII, 3 (1983), 25.

4 H.H. Gerth and C. Wright Mills, eds., *From Max Weber: Essays in Sociology* (New York: Oxford University Press, 1947), 196–8.

5 F.C. Okoli, 'The Dilemma of Premature Bureaucratization in the New States of Africa', *African Studies Review*, XXIII, 2 (1980), 1–16.

6 *Ibid*, 11.

7 G.E. Caiden and N.J. Caiden, 'Administrative Corruption', *Public Administration Review*, XXXVII, 3 (1977), 306.

8 Y.-A. Fauré and J.-F. Médard, 'Introduction', *État et Bourgeoisie en Côte d'Ivoire* (Paris: Karthala, 1982), 17.

9 J.-F. Médard, 'La regulation socio-politique', in *ibid*, 76–7.

10 *Africa Confidential*, XXIII, 19 (22 September 1982), 1, 4.

11 United Nations, *Survey of Economic Conditions in Africa, 1972* (New York: United Nations, 1973), 75.

12 *Ibid*, 233.

13 M.N. Ogbonna, 'Tax Evasion in Nigeria', *Africa Today*, XXII, 1 (1975), 55.

14 On parastatals in general, see Goran Hyden, *No Shortcuts to Progress* (London: Heinemann, 1983), 99. On the Ivory Coast, see H.S. Marcussen, 'The Ivory Coast Facing the Economic Crisis', in Jerker Carlssen, ed., *Recession in Africa* (Uppsala: Scandinavian Institute of African Studies, 1983), 10–11.

15 Y.-A. Fauré, 'Le complexe politico-économique', in Fauré and Médard, *État et bourgeoisie*, 55.

16 All quotes are from A.C.I. Mbanefo, 'The Management of Public Enterprises' Control and Autonomy – External and Internal Problems', in A.H. Rweyamamu and G. Hyden, eds., *A Decade of Public Administration in Africa* (Nairobi: East African Literature Bureau, 1975), 289–99.

17 E.J. Wilson, 'Public Corporation Expansion in Nigeria', in Pearl Robinson and Elliot Skinner, eds., *Transformation and Resiliency in*

Africa (Washington, D.C.: Howard University Press, 1983), 45–68.

18 This paragraph draws on C. Kirkpatrick and F. Nixson, 'Transnational Corporations and Economic Development', *Journal of Modern African Studies*, XIX, 3 (1981), 375–8.

19 See T. Turner, 'Multinational Corporations and the Instability of the Nigerian State', *Review of African Political Economy*, 5 (1976), 63–79; and T. Turner, 'The Transfer of Oil Technology and the Nigerian State', *Development and Change*, VII, 4 (1976), 353–90.

20 D.J. Gould, 'The Administration of Underdevelopment', in Guy Gran, ed., *Zaire: The Political Economy of Underdevelopment* (New York: Praeger, 1979), 98–9.

21 T.J. Biersteker, 'Indigenization in Nigeria: Renationalization or Denationalization?', in I. William Zartman, ed., *The Political Economy of Nigeria* (New York: Praeger, 1983), 185.

22 These strategies are described in *ibid.*, 185–206; and A. Hoogvelt, 'Indigenization and Foreign Capital: Industrialization in Nigeria', *Review of African Political Economy*, 14 (1979), 56–68.

23 Biersteker, 'Indigenisation in Nigeria', 202.

24 L.L. Rood, 'Nationalisation and Indigenisation in Africa', *Journal of Modern African Studies*, XIV, 3 (1976), 429–37.

25 For these practices, see S.P. Schatz, 'Crude Private Neo-Imperialism: A New Pattern in Africa', *Journal of Modern African Studies*, VII, 4 (1969), 677–88.

26 For a case study of these problems, see J. Loxley and J.S. Saul, 'Multinationals, Workers and Parastatals in Tanzania', *Review of African Political Economy*, 2 (1975), 54–88.

27 The president mentioned this in a speech to the PDCI's Political Bureau, the text of which appeared in the official daily, *Fraternité-Matin*. See *Africa Confidential*, XXIV, 10 (11 May 1983), 8.

28 See H.H. Werlin, 'The Consequences of Corruption: The Ghanaian Experience', *Political Science Quarterly*, LXXXVIII, 1 (1973), 73–5.

29 R.H. Green, 'Magendo in the Political Economy of Uganda'. Discussion Paper 164, Institute for Development Studies, University of Sussex, August 1981, 5.

30 See O.J. Igué, 'L'officiel, la parallèlle et le clandestin: commerce et intégration en Afrique de l'Ouest', *Politique Africaine*, 9 (1983), 29–51.

31 *Ibid.*

32 Naomi Chazan, *An Anatomy of Ghanaian Politics: Managing Political Recession, 1969–1982* (Boulder, Col.: Westview Press, 1983), 195.

33 G. Prunier, 'Le Magendo: Essai sur quelques aspects marginaux des échanges commerciaux en Afrique orientale', *Politique Africaine*, 9 (1983), 53–62.

34 Green, 'Magendo', 9.

7 SURVIVAL STRATEGIES

1 World Bank, *Accelerated Development in Sub-Saharan Africa: An Agenda for Action* (Washington, D.C.: World Bank, August 1981), p.1.10.

2 Information on Ghana is drawn mainly from Naomi Chazan, *An Anatomy of Ghanaian Politics: Managing Political Recession, 1969–1982* (Boulder, Col.: Westview Press, 1983), 198–9.

3 Information on Tanzania provided for Dr Mutahaba of the University of Dar es Salaam on 23 February 1984.

4 Manfred Max-Neef, *From the Outside Looking In: Experiences in 'Barefoot Economics'* (Uppsala: Dag Hammarskjold Foundation, 1982), 117.

5 See D. Goulet, 'Development as Liberation: Policy Lessons From Case Studies', *World Development*, VII, 6 (1979), 555–66.

6 See, e.g., a report on the role of Canadian NGOs by the Science Council of Canada, entitled *From the Bottom Up: Involvement of Canadian NGOs in Food and Rural Development in the Third World* (Ottawa: Science Council of Canada, June 1979).

7 For the data, see C. Colclough, 'Are African Governments as Unproductive as the Accelerated Development Report Implies?', *Institute for Development Studies Bulletin*, XIV, 1 (1983), 24–9.

8 Goran Hyden, *No Shortcuts to Progress: African Development Management in Perspective* (London: Heinemann, 1983).

GUIDE TO FURTHER READING

These studies pertain to the major themes in each chapter. The list is biased in favour of items that are already published, readily available, and written in English. However, works that are highly pertinent or seminal are included regardless of these criteria.

OF GENERAL RELEVANCE

Austin, Dennis. *Politics in Africa*. 2nd ed. Hanover, N.H.: University Press of New England, 1984.

Chazan, Naomi. *An Anatomy of Ghanaian Politics: Managing Political Recession, 1969–1982*. Boulder, Col.: Westview, 1983.

Davidson, Basil. *Let Freedom Come: Africa in Modern History*. Boston: Little, Brown, 1978.

Hyden, Goran. *No Shortcuts to Progress: African Development Management in Perspective*. London: Heinemann, and Los Angeles: University of California Press, 1983.

I DISAPPOINTMENTS OF INDEPENDENCE

Austin, Dennis. 'Things Fall Apart?', *Orbis*, xxv, 4 (1982), 925–47.

Carlsson, Jerker, ed. *Recession in Africa*. Uppsala: Scandinavian Institute of African Studies, 1983.

Lemarchand, René. 'Quelles Indépendences?', *Le Mois en Afrique* (Fév.–Mars, 1983), 19–37.

Liser, F.B. 'A Basic Needs Strategy and the Physical Quality of Life Index (PQLI): Africa's Development Prospects', in Timothy M. Shaw, ed., *Alternative Futures for Africa*. Boulder, Col.: Westview, 1982, 201–36.

Roemer, M. 'Economic Development in Africa: Performance Since Independence and a Strategy for the Future', *Daedalus*, CXI, 2 (1982), 125–48.

'What Prospects for African Economic Development?', special issue of *Africa Report*, XXVIII, 5 (1983).

2 WHY CAPITALISM FAILS

Anell, Lars and Birgitta Nygren. *The Developing Countries and the World Economic Order*. London: Methuen, 1980.

Bayart, J.-F. 'La revanche des sociétés africaines', *Politique Africaine*, 11 (Sept. 1983), 95–127.

Beckman, B. 'Imperialism and the "National Bourgeois"', *Review of African Political Economy*, 22 (1981), 5–19.

'Whose State? State and Capitalist Development in Nigeria', *Review of African Political Economy*, 23 (1982), 37–51.

Griffin, Keith. 'The International Transmission of Inequality', in Griffin, *International Inequality and National Poverty*. London: Macmillan, 1978, 13–41.

Kamarick, A.M. 'The Resources of Tropical Africa', *Daedalus*, CXI, 2 (1982), 149–64.

Langdon, S. and L.K. Mytelka. 'Africa in the Changing World Economy', in Colin Legum *et al, Africa in the 1980s*. New York: McGraw-Hill, 1979, 123–211.

Leys, Colin. 'African Economic Development in Theory and Practice', *Daedalus*, CXI 2 (1982), 99–124.

Marcussen, Henrik S. and Jens E. Torp. *Internationalization of Capital: Prospects for the Third World: Case Study of the Ivory Coast*. London: Zed Press, 1982.

Munro, J. Forbes. *Africa and the International Economy, 1800–1960*. Totowa, N.J.: Rowman and Littlefield, 1976.

Myrdal, Gunnar. 'The "Soft" State', in his *The Challenge of World Poverty*. N.Y.: Vintage Books, 1970, 208–52.

Smith, Tony. *The Pattern of Imperialism: The US, Great Britain and the Late-Industrializing World Since 1815*. Cambridge University Press, 1981.

Supple, Barry. 'The State and the Industrial Revolution', in C.M. Cippola, ed., *The Fontana Economic History of Europe*, vol. 3, London: Fontana, 1973, 301–57.

Wallerstein, I. 'The Three Stages of African Involvement in the World Economy', in P.C.W. Gutkind and Immanuel Wallerstein, eds., *The Political Economy of Contemporary Africa*. Beverly Hills, Calif.: Sage, 1978, 30–57.

Wheeler, D. 'Sources of stagnation in Sub-Saharan Africa,' *World Development*, XII, 1 (1984), 1–24.

3 COLONIAL ROOTS OF THE CONTEMPORARY CRISIS

Brett, E.A. *Colonialism and Underdevelopment in East Africa, 1919–39*. London: Heinemann Educational Books, 1973.

Fortes, Meyer and E.E. Evans-Pritchard, eds. *African Political Systems*. London: Oxford University Press, 1940.

Gann, Lewis H. and Peter Duignan, eds. *Colonialism in Africa, 1870–1914*: vol. I: *History and Politics of Colonialism, 1870–1914*. Cambridge University Press, 1969.

Good, K. 'Settler Colonialism: Economic Development and Class Formation', *Journal of Modern African Studies*, XIV, 4 (1976), 597–620.

Hodgkin, Thomas. *Nationalism in Colonial Africa*. New York University Press, 1957.

Kilson, M.L., Jr. 'Nationalism and Social Classes in British West Africa', in Immanuel Wallerstein, ed., *Social Change: The Colonial Situation*. New York: John Wiley & Son, 1966, 533–50.

Post, Ken. '"Peasantisation" and Rural Political Movements in West Africa', *European Journal of Sociology*, XIII, 2 (1972), 223–54.

Robinson, Ronald. 'Non-European Foundations of European Imperialism: Sketch for a Theory of Collaboration', in Robert Owen and Bob Sutcliffe, eds., *Studies in the Theory of Imperialism*. London: Longmans, 1972, 117–40.

Wallerstein, I. 'Class, Tribe and Party in West Africa', in Seymour M. Lipset and Stein Rokkan, eds., *Party Systems and Voter Alignments*. New York: Free Press, 1967, 497–518.

'Elites in French-Speaking West Africa: The Social Basis of Ideas', *Journal of Modern African Studies*, III, 1 (1965), 1–33.

4 CLASS, TRIBE AND POLITICS

Bates, Robert. 'Modernization, Ethnic Competition and the Rationality of Politics in Contemporary Africa', in Donald Rothchild and

Victor Olorunsola, eds., *State vs. Ethnic Claims: African Policy Dilemmas*. Boulder, Col.: Westview Press, 1983, 152–71.

Brown, David. 'Who are the Tribalists? Social Pluralism and Political Ideology in Ghana', *African Affairs*, 322 (Jan. 1982), 37–69.

Buijtenhuijs, R. 'The Revolutionary Potential of Black Africa: Dissident Elites', *African Perspectives*, 2 (1978), 135–46.

Connor, W. 'Nation-Building or Nation-Destroying?', *World Politics*, XXIV, 3 (1972), 319–55.

Fauré, Y.-A. et J.-F. Médard. *État et bourgeoisie en Côte d'Ivoire*. Paris: Éditions Karthala, 1982.

Hobsbawm, E.J. 'Class Consciousness in History', in Istvan Meszaros, ed., *Aspects of History and Class Consciousness*. London: RKP, 1971, 5–21.

Kasfir, Nelson. *The Shrinking Political Arena: Participation and Ethnicity in African Politics*. Los Angeles: University of California Press, 1976.

Lemarchand, René. 'The State and Society in Africa: Ethnic Stratification and Restratification in Historical and Comparative Perspective', in Donald Rothchild and Victor Olorunsola, eds., *State versus Ethnic Claims: African Policy Dilemmas*. Boulder, Col.: Westview Press, 1983, 44–66.

Melson, Robert and Howard Wolpe. 'Modernization and the Politics of Communalism: A Theoretical Perspective', *American Political Science Review*, LXIV (Dec. 1970), 112–30.

Sandbrook, Richard and Robin Cohen, eds. *The Development of an African Working Class*. London: Longmans, and Toronto: University of Toronto Press, 1975.

Saul, John S. 'The Dialectics of Class and Tribe', in his *The State and Revolution in East Africa*. New York: MR Press, 1979, 391–423.

Sklar, Richard. 'The Nature of Class Domination in Africa', *Journal of Modern African Studies*, XVII, 4 (1979), 531–52.

Swainson, Nicola. 'State and Economy in Post-Colonial Kenya, 1963-78', *Canadian Journal of African Studies*, XII, 3 (1978), 357–81.

Welch, Claude F. 'Obstacles to "Peasant War" in Africa', *African Studies Review*, XX, 3 (1977), 121–30.

Young, Crawford. 'Patterns of Social Conflict: State, Class and Ethnicity', *Daedalus*, CXI, 2 (1982), 71–98.

5 ANATOMY OF PERSONAL RULE

Bowman, L.W. and J.A. Lefebvre. 'US Strategic Policy in Northeast Africa and the Indian Ocean', *Africa Report*, XXXVIII, 6 (1983), 4–9.

Chazan, N. 'The New Politics of Participation in Tropical Africa', *Comparative Politics*, XIV, 2 (1982), 169–89.

Cheche, Kenya. *Independent Kenya*. London: Zed Press, 1983.

Enloe, Cynthia H. *Police, Military and Ethnicity: Foundations of State Power*. New Brunswick, N.J.: Transaction Books, 1980.

Flynn, P. 'Class, Clientelism and Coercion: Some Mechanisms of Internal Dependency and Control', *Journal of Commonwealth and Comparative Political Studies*, XII, 2 (1974), 133–56.

Gavshon, Arthur. *Crisis in Africa: Battleground of East and West*. Harmondsworth: Pelican Books, 1981.

Gran, Guy, ed. *Zaire: The Political Economy of Underdevelopment*. New York: Praeger, 1979. (See in particular articles by Gran and D.J. Gould.)

Jackson, Robert and Carl Rosberg. *Personal Rule in Black Africa*. Los Angeles: University of California Press, 1982.

Klare, Michael. *Beyond the 'Vietnam Syndrome': US Intervention in the 1980s*. Washington, D.C.: Institute for Policy Studies, 1982.

Klare, Michael and Cynthia Arnson. *Supplying Repression: US Support for Authoritarian Regimes Abroad*. Washington, D.C.: Institute for Policy Studies, 1981.

Lemarchand, René. 'Comparative Political Clientelism', in S.N. Eisenstadt and R. Lemarchand, eds., *Political Clientelism, Patronage and Development*. Beverly Hills, Calif.: Sage Publishers, 1981, 7–29.

'The CIA in Africa: How Central? How Intelligent?', *Journal of Modern African Studies*, XIV, 3 (1976), 401–26.

Le Vine, V.T. 'African Patrimonial Regimes in Comparative Perspective', *Journal of Modern African Studies*, XV, 4 (1980), 657–73.

Luckham, Robin. 'French Militarism in Africa', *Review of African Political Economy*, 24 (1982), 55–84.

Mowoe, Isaac J., ed. *The Performance of Soldiers as Governors: African Politics and the African Military*. Washington, D.C.: University Press of America, 1980. (Case studies of Benin, Congo, Ethiopia, Ghana, Mali, Nigeria, Sierra Leone, Uganda, Zaire.)

Owusu, Maxwell. *Uses and Abuses of Political Power: A Case Study of Continuity and Change in the Politics of Ghana*. Chicago: University of Chicago Press, 1970.

Price, Robert. 'Politics and Culture in Contemporary Ghana: The Big-Man, Small-Boy Syndrome', *Journal of African Studies*, 2 (1974), 173–204.

Stockwell, John. *In Search of Enemies: A CIA Story*. New York: Norton, 1977.

Szeftel, M. 'Political Graft and the Spoils System in Zambia', *Review of African Political Economy*, 24 (1982), 4–21.

Weissman, S. 'CIA Covert Actions in Zaire and Angola: Patterns and Consequences', *Political Science Quarterly*, XCIV, 2 (1979), 263–86.

Willame, Jean-Claude. *Patrimonialism and Political Change in the Congo* [Zaire]. Stanford: Stanford University Press, 1971.

6 THE DOWNWARD SPIRAL

Biersteker, T.J. 'Indigenization in Nigeria: Renationalization or Denationalization?', in I.W. Zartman, ed., *The Political Economy of Nigeria*. New York: Praeger, 1983, 185–206.

Caiden, G.E. and N.J. Caiden. 'Administrative Corruption', *Public Administration Review*, XXXVII, 3 (1977), 301–9.

Collins, Paul. 'The Management and Administration of Parastatal Organizations for the Promotion of Indigenous Enterprise: A West African Experience', *Public Administration and Development*, 1, 2 (1981), 121–32.

Gould, D.J. 'The Administration of Underdevelopment', in Guy Gran, ed., *Zaire: The Political Economy of Underdevelopment*. New York: Praeger, 1979, 87–107.

Gutteridge, William F. *Military Regimes in Africa*. London: Methuen, 1975.

Hirschmann, David. 'Development or Underdevelopment Administration? A Further "Deadlock"', *Development and Change*, XII, 3 (1981), 459–79.

Igué, O.J. 'L'officiel, le parallèle et le clandestin: commerce et intégration en Afrique de l'Ouest', *Politique Africaine*, 9 (1983), 29–51.

Kaplinsky, Raphael. 'Export-Oriented Growth: A Large International

Firm in a Small Developing Country [Kenya]', *World Development*, VII, 8/9 (1979), 825–34.

Kirkpatrick, C. and F. Nixson. 'Transnational Corporations and Economic Development', *Journal of Modern African Studies*, XIX, 3 (1981), 367–99.

Langdon, Steven. 'Multinational Corporations, Taste Transfer and Underdevelopment: A Case Study from Kenya', *Review of African Political Economy*, 2 (1975), 12–35.

Loxley, John and John S. Saul. 'Multinationals, Workers and Parastatals in Tanzania', *Review of African Political Economy*, 2 (1975), 54–88.

Lungu, Gatian and John Oni. 'Administrative Weakness in Contemporary Africa', *Africa Quarterly*, XVIII, 4 (1979), 3–16.

MacGaffey, Janet. 'How to Survive and Become Rich Amidst Devastation: The Second Economy in Zaire', *African Affairs*, LXXXII, 328 (1983), 351–66.

Okoli, Fidelis C. 'The Dilemma of Premature Bureaucratization in the New States of Africa: The Case of Nigeria', *African Studies Review*, XXIII, 2 (1980), 1–16.

Prunier, G. 'Le magendo: essai sur quelques aspects marginaux des échanges commerciaux en Afrique orientale', *Politique Africaine*, 9 (1983), 53–62.

Rood, Leslie L. 'Nationalization and Indigenization in Africa', *Journal of Modern African Studies*, XIV, 3 (1976), 427–47.

Rweyamamu, Anthony and Goran Hyden. *A Decade of Public Administration in Africa*. Nairobi: East African Literature Bureau, 1975. (See especially the five chapters on the problems and prospects of public corporations in various African countries.)

Turner, Terisa. 'Multinational Corporations and the Instability of the Nigerian State', *Review of African Political Economy*, 5 (1976), 63–79.

Turok, Ben. 'Control in the Parastatal Sector of Zambia', *Journal of Modern African Studies*, XIX, 3 (1981), 421–45.

Werlin, Herbert. 'The Roots of Corruption – The Ghanaian Enquiry', *Journal of Modern African Studies*, X, 2 (1972), 247–66.

'The Consequences of Corruption: The Ghanaian Experience', *Political Science Quarterly*, LXXXVIII, 1 (1973), 71–85.

Wilson, E. J. 'Public Corporation Expansion in Nigeria', in Pearl Robinson and Elliot Skinner, eds., *Transformation and Resiliency in Africa*. Washington, D.C.: Howard University Press, 1983, 45–68.

7 SURVIVAL STRATEGIES

Goulet, Denis. 'Development as Liberation: Policy Lessons from Case Studies', *World Development*, VII, 6 (1979), 555–66.

Gran, Guy. *Development by People*. New York: Praeger, 1983.

Sandbrook, Richard. *The Politics of Basic Needs: Urban Aspects of Assaulting Poverty in Africa*. London: Heinemann, and Toronto: University of Toronto Press, 1982.

Streeten, Paul. 'Approaches to a New International Economic Order', *World Development*, X, 1 (1982), 1–18.

World Bank. *Accelerated Development in Sub-Saharan Africa: An Agenda for Action*. Washington, D.C.: World Bank, September 1981.

Towards Sustained Development in Sub-Saharan Africa: A Joint Program of Action. Washington, D.C.: World Bank, September 1984.

INDEX

Farm Labour

KEN SWINDELL

Senior Lecturer, Department of Geography, University of Birmingham

This book highlights the most important attributes of farm labour in Africa and places them within a context of historical change. International trade, colonialism, transport and the growth of towns have all exerted a powerful influence on rural Africa. More recently post-colonial states have attempted to reshape agriculture and transform rural societies. Yet agriculture is still dominated by small commodity producers who have retained control over their means of production, and it has not lost its labour-intensive character. Many small farmers now produce for local or international markets and this has been achieved by new patterns of work and labour organisation. Domestic production and family labour have been expanded or reduced by the spread of hired labour, as workers are redistributed between richer and poorer farmers and developed and underdeveloped regions. In addition, women have become more important as field labourers, as off-farm work for men becomes part of household reproduction.

Migrant Laborers

SHARON STICHTER

Associate Professor of Sociology, University of Massachusetts-Boston

This book surveys the literature on labour migration in east, west and southern Africa and interprets it from a political economy perspective. It addresses the controversies as to the origins of migrancy and its effects on the rural economy, emphasizing the differences in the response of various African precapitalist societies to wage labour, and the regional variations in the effects on the rural economy and on the division of labour within the rural household. Male migrants' experiences with forced labour, recruitment systems, advance payments, and compound controls are described, and the rather different character of women's migration is examined.

A central concern is the development of migrant workers' consciousness and forms of resistance. Labour protest among dockers, miners and domestic workers is examined and, finally, the persistence of migrancy in South Africa today is contrasted with the decline of labour migrancy in other parts of the continent.